The Blueprint To Hacking

Beginners Guide to Ethical Computer Hacking!

By: Cyber Punk Architects

About CyberPunk Architects

Computer programming doesn't have to be complicated. When you start with the basics its actually quite simple. That is what Cyberpunk Architects are all about. We take pride in giving people the *blueprint* for everything related to computer programming and computer programming languages. We include Python programming, Raspberry Pi, SQL, Java, HTML and a lot more.

We take a sophisticated approach and teach you everything you need to know from the ground up. Starting with a strong base is the only way you will truly master the art of computer programming. We understand that it can be challenging to find the right way to learn the often complex field of programming especially for those who are not tech savvy. Our team at Cyberpunk Architects is dedicated to helping you achieve your goals when it comes to computer programming.

We are here to provide you with the *blueprint* to give you a strong foundation so you can build on that and go into any area of programming that you wish. Our architects are comprised of professionals who have been in the industry of information technology for decades and have a passion for teaching and helping others especially through our books. They are friendly, experienced, knowledgeable computer programmers who love sharing their vast knowledge with anyone who has an interest in it.

We look forward to getting a chance to work with you soon. Here at Cyberpunk Architects, you can always be sure that you are working with right people. Allow us take care of your needs for learning computer programming. If

you have any questions about the services that
we are providing, please do not hesitate to get
in touch with us right away.

Check out all of our books at:

Bit.ly/Cyberpunkbooks

As a THANK YOU for purchasing our books we want to give you **a free bonus**. **A quick guide on how to get started with programming**. This book covers the basics of what you want to know to get started.

Free Bonus!

Programing can be hard but it doesn't have to be! Take this free PDF guide to understand some of the basics of programming

Download the free guide:

bit.ly/cpfreeguide

Book 1

The Blueprint To Hacking

Book 2

The Blueprint to Raspberry Pi 3

Book 3

The Blueprint To Python Programming

Table Of Contents

Introduction

With today's high level of technological culture and massive development of information technology, there is no surprise many people see their future in this field of industry. This type of science, information science is desirable and available to broad masses of people. By knowing the real power of information technology, you will be able to manipulate, store and study many different types of data from the comfort of your home.

In the world, there are many undergraduate degree programs preparing students to work in this field of industry on many different levels. IT specialists work for huge companies and are responsible for network administration and software development, increasing productivity and efficiency.

On the other hand, there is huge subculture

involving people who are accessing online databases, manipulating and overcoming limitations of the software. By overcoming the obstacles and limitations of programming systems, you will be able to engage in advanced studies of software and operating systems. You will enter into a different world of information technology.

This book is about ethical computer hacking, so we will discuss hacking only in an ethical manner. Hacker ethic allows you to manipulate software in no harmful way, to share information to the world that is not damaging in any way. This guide will teach you how to access computers and information that can benefit you and others as well.

We all know that knowledge should be shared, especially knowledge that can be helpful and can improve our personal knowledge. Information should be available to everybody, and all information should be free. Today computers are life changing and take a huge part in everybody's life. This ethical beginner's guide to hacking computer will be your card into the power of information technology.

There is a common goal, many principles and values of hacker ethic are based on this common goal. By using the knowledge of hacking, you will be able to create something completely new and interesting. You will be able to access computers, learn about operating systems and share information to the world. You will see limitless opportunities in the information sector and be amazed by the greatness and power of one single information.

Ethical ideas and values of this subculture have constructive goal, and there is always feeling of right and wrong present. Only ethical hacking is right and no damaging in any way. In order to overcome obstacles of hacking, first of all, you will need to be online. Besides being online you will need operating system Linux, most of the internet sites run Linux operating system.

I will later explain how to use Linux Terminal. You need to have point to point protocol internet connection. Most of DLS connections are fortunately point to point protocol. If you don't have PPP (point to point protocol) contact your internet service provider and tell them you are interested in getting PPP.

All of these steps will be explained later step by step, but you should know that hacking isn't easy job. It demands constant learning and adoption of new knowledge. Learning and discovering is an essential thing when it comes to hacking. It will take you a certain number of hours on computer each day.

Before going into world of hacking, you should be familiar with programming languages and have certain programming skills. There are many programming languages, and I recommend Python because It is simple and easy to use. There are great tutorials about programming with Python, so you don't need to spend extra money on books. Besides Python later you should be learning other programming languages like C and C++, they are very difficult to learn, but at some point, you will be able to use them after learning the basics of Python.

We will discuss these basic steps later in details. First, you need to know there are many different types of hackers and many reasons why people enter the world of hacking. You should be familiar with these types of hackers even though this is such a stereotypical view.

1. **Script Kiddie** is the type I am mentioning first. This is normally amateur hacker who breaks into people's

computers and have poor knowledge of information technology. Script Kiddie use prepackaged automatic scripts and software created by real hackers. They are copying codes from these automatic scripts; they just download prepared software in order to put a virus or something else harmful. Basically, they watch YouTube tutorials on how to use these scripts. They flood an IP address with huge amount of information, and it collapses.

2. **White Hat** is known as ethical hacker. Many of White Hat hackers have college degree in IT technology and security. They have non-malevolent and no damaging purpose. They are helping people fight against other hackers, help them remove viruses or PenTest companies. White Hat is by all standards ethical and moral programmer.

3. **Black Hat**are the third type of hackers, commonly known as crackers. They surf the internet and discover weak frameworks. They are using basic and common hacking techniques to steal money and information from banks and companies with weak security systems.

4. **Grey Hat** is another type of hacker.bGrey Hat is breaking into computers with weak security, breaking into PC frameworks. Gray Hat hackers are using many different strategies in order to extort Mastercard, many other types of vandalism and various types of information stealing.

5. **Green Hat**are hackers really into hacking. They want to learn and discover always, and that is why they may be asking many basic questions. They are

listening with great devotion and curiosity.

Elite hacker is above the average in the hacking world, really devoted with great social status among the others. They are treated as special in the subculture of hacking. They are masters of discovering and inventing new things. Masters with solid reputation among the people, cream of the hacker world.

These are the most relevant types of hackers. This guide is about ethical hacking so you should use your knowledge only for moral and ethical purposes.

Chapter 1: How To Setup Your New Hacking Environment

It is impossible to learn everything about hacking; there is huge amount of information on the computers. People usually tend to specialize in one specific field when it comes to hacking such as software development, computer security or networking. It is a bit early for you as a beginner to think about specializing in any of these fields. You should first learn basic techniques and strategies when it comes to hacking. Later in future, you will have clearer mind about your possibilities.

Discovering and knowing what is going on inside the computer system is an essential thing, this is common goal of all hackers. By knowing what is going on inside the system, you will be able to manipulate and modify information for better. You are going to create something completely new that fits your needs. Learning about hacking is gaining access into powerful system of information and technology.

Knowledge will always be the most powerful thing, and power has been used both in good and wrong things. We will just focus on knowledge for moral and ethical purposes that benefit many people.

Here are the steps you should take to get started:

1. You have already taken the first step into the world of hacking by showing an interest and curiosity to learn about hacking.

2. Like I mentioned before, the second step is knowing the basics of programming languages. Programming skills and techniques are going to be the most valuable

you have for hacking. A programming language is designed to give instructions to the machines, especially computers. With the programming languages, you can create different programs and control the behavior of the computer. You should start with something simple like creative website or create application for smartphone.

Where and which programming languages to learn?

On the internet, there are many great tutorials about using programming languages. You can watch video tutorial as well. You shouldn't forget about library. There you can find tons of books about programming and networking. Besides video tutorials and books, there are plenty sites on the internet with step by step guides about programming.

- Java is one of the longest influential

programming languages, great for beginners. It lets you think like real hacker, to think logically. Besides Java I mentioned before Python, it is open and free to use. It will teach you really useful strategies, modularity, and indentation.

3. For the perfect hacking environment, you will need certain devices. Like I said before you have to be able to be online and have point to point protocol. If you don't have one you should contact your internet provider, but don't worry, almost every DLS internet connection has PPP. Other important things are you should have some knowledge about network ports, common network protocols, HTTP and you should know how each of these things works.

4. You will need operating system that is convenient for programming. Unix operating system is perfect and suitable for

hackers all over the world. Unix operating system can develop and create software that can be run on other systems as well. You can use a great number of software tools. Unix consists of many great utilities such as a master program kernel. Unix emerged as important learning and teaching tools when it comes to computer technology.

- Besides unix operating system, you will need shell account. A shell account is user account that runs on the remote server under the Unix operating system. It gives you access to a shell via different kinds of protocols. Shell accounts have been used for file storage, software development or web space.

- You will also need a Unix box. It is a computer that runs any of the several Unix operating systems like Linux. This term Unix box came in order to distinguish Unix operating system and more common Windows operating system. Unix operating system and Unix computer are able to differentiate many different servers quickly. Unix computers are perfect for security administration as well as for hacking. The most important thing is that most internet websites are running Unix operating system.

- In order to obtain Unix operating system, you will have to buy one or get free versions. I recommend Linux operating system or BSD. Linux is more suitable for beginners because it is easy to use, so you should consider buying Linux first. You can buy Linux set online from many different sites. There are many free versions of Linux; you will just need to find someone with this operating system to burn it for your personal use. Don't worry, Linux is free for distribution, and it's not illegal to makes copies.

- When it comes to installing Linux operating system, don't worry, it is quite easy. You can find complete guides and video tutorials on the internet with the installation instructions. Just type into search engine Linux installation, you will get all of the information that you need.

Reminder: In order to hack and manipulate the software, you have to be able to be online using Linux operating system. Like I mentioned before, you need point to point protocol internet connection. Almost all of the DLS connections are point to point protocol, but on the other hand, dial-up is not PPP. If you have DLS connection, you are lucky, and there is no need to worry about anything. You are ready for some hacking.

5. After you get these stuff, it is time to pick books about Linux operating system or any other operating system you may be using. I recommend you books with step by step guides for beginners. Your local library has plenty of books about computer technology; it won't be a problem finding any particular one you need. For me personally, the best book about Linux is Running Linux written by Matt Welsh. It is really for beginners in computer technology. If you are maybe using other Unix versions of operating system, I warmly recommend any book from O'Reilly Collection. I find them perfect for beginners.

You have to keep in mind constantly that hacking is hard work, constant learning about information and computer science in different and intriguing ways. You just made your first step; you are intrigued by hacking world, you want to know about manipulating software, creating something completely new from information you get. That is the most important step, wanting to know more. You should keep in mind that hacking is huge devotion, you will need to expand your limits and knowledge. The most important thing is learning, so you have to read a lot about information and computer technology, search online for your many questions, visit forums about hacking. After setting up perfect environment for hacking, we should start with basics.

Chapter 2: How To Use The Linux Terminal And Master Its Functions

As I mentioned before, Linus is Unix-like computer operating system; it is developed under the version of the free and open-source software. Unix operating systems are free for distribution and development. The most important component of Linux operating system is Linux kernel. Originally Linux was developed for personal use and computers, but since then Linux has been developing many other platforms, more than any other operating system. Today Linux is the most used operating system in the world, has the largest installed base of all operating systems and is leading operating system on many servers and desktop computers. Today many smartphones run Linux components and derivatives.

The greatest example of free and open-source software is absolutely the development of Linux operating system. Source codes may be distributed and modified by anyone by the certain terms and licenses. You can use find many popular mainstream Linux versions such as Fedora, Linux Mint or Ubuntu. You have plenty options. Besides these versions, you can find for free supporting utilities, large amount of applications and software supporting Linux operating system. All of these have supporting role in distribution's intended use.

Linux is high-level assembly, and programming language freely redistributed and with easy porting to any computer platform. For this reason, Unix-like operating system Linux quickly became adopted by academic circles and institutions. Today it is widely used and distributed all over the world. Linux is the result of the project of creating Unix-like operating system with completely free software. It is opponent to the Microsoft's monopoly in the desktop computer technology. Linux today is more used in the field of embedded systems and supercomputers.

Linux is modular operating system; device drivers are integrated or added like modules while the system is running. Some of the Linux components include C standard library, widget toolkits, and software libraries. This guide will help you and guide you through the Linux terminal commands and basics. Linux Terminal is really powerful tool, and you shouldn't be afraid to use it.

Learning the Linux basics is first and crucial step into the world of hacking. In this guide, we have to cover topics such as Linux command line and Linux executing commands. These are basics when it comes to the Linux operating system. You should familiarize yourself with the Linux Terminal emulator in the first place. It will become very easy to use when we pass through the basics first. It is needless to say you have to be able to connect to the Linux server.

At the very beginning, we should distinguish what the terminal emulator is. Terminal emulator is the program allowing the usage of terminal in a graphical environment. Today many people use operating system with graphical user interface and terminal emulator is an essential feature for Linux users. Besides Linux, you can find terminal emulator program in other operating systems such as Mac OS X and Windows. Here we are going to discuss Linux Terminal emulator.

You should be familiar with the shell. When it comes to the Linux, the shell is standing for command-line interface. The shell reads and interprets commands from the user. It reads script files and tells the operating system what to do with the obtained scripts. There are many widely used shells such as C shell or Bourne shell. Every shell has its own features, but many of the shells feature some same characteristics. Each shell function in the same way of input and output direction and condition-testing. Bourne-Again shell is the default shell for almost every Linux version.

Another important thing is knowledge of command prompt. The message of the day is the first thing you will see when you log in to server. It is message containing information about the version of Linux you a recurrently using. After the message of the day, you will be directed into the shell prompt known as command prompt. In the command prompt, you will give directions and tasks to the server. You will see information ate the shell prompt, and these information can be modified and customized by the users. In the command prompt, you are able to manipulate the information.

You may be logged into the shell prompt as root. In the Linux operating system, the root user is the special user who is able to perform administrative tasks and functions of the operating system. Super user account has permission to perform unrestricted commands to the server. As a super user, you have limitless powers when it comes to the manipulating commands given to the server. You will be able to give unrestricted administrative tasks and commands.

Besides shell prompt, we should discuss executing commands as well. You give commands to the server in the shell prompt. You specify the name of the files both as script of binary program. With the operating system Linux, there are already many utilities installed previously. These utilities let you navigate through the file system, install applications and configure the system. Giving tasks and commands in the shell prompt is called the process.

By giving directions in the command prompt, you are able to install software package and navigate through the system. When you are executing the commands in the foreground, you have to wait for the process to be finished before going to the shell prompt. This default way of commands being executed is case-sensitive including all names and files, commands and options. If something is not working as planned, you should double-check the spelling and case of all your commands.

You may have problems while connecting to the Linux server, online you can find solution to the problem with the connection. In order to execute the command free of arguments and options, you just simply type name of the command and press return. Commands like this, without arguments and options, behave differently from the commands with arguments. The behavior of the outcome varies from each command.

When it comes to the commands with arguments and options, accepting arguments and options can change the overall performance of the command. Every argument specifies and directs the command in a certain way. For example, a cd is the component of the command and arguments follows the certain command. Options that follows commands are known as flags.

Options are nothing more than special arguments directed in a certain way. They also affect and modify the behavior at the command prompt space. Same as arguments, options follow the commands and can contain more than one options for the same command. Options are single-character special arguments usually having descriptive character. Both arguments and options contain additional information about the commands and about each file and script. They can be combined into certain groups of options and arguments while running commands at the command prompt.

We should pay attention to the environment variables as well. Environment variables can change behavior of the commands and the ways of the command execution. First when you log in to server, default environment valuables will be set already according to configuration files. You can see at the command prompt all environment variables sessions by running env command. After running any command, next step is looking for path entry. The path will give you all the directions about the shell looking for executable programs and scripts.

From command prompt, you can retrieve the values of environment variables just by prefixing name of the variable with $character. By doing this, you will expand variable to its value. IF you see an empty string, you are probably trying to access variable which hasn't been set yet. In that case, you will get empty string.

Now that you are familiar with the environment variables you are able to set them. For setting environment variable you need to type variable name followed by an = sign. Finally, you should type the desired value. The original value of the variable will be overwritten if you are setting the existing environment variable and if the variable doesn't exist by doing this, it will be created. Command export allows you to export variables inherited during the process. To be more clear, you can use any script from the exported variable from current process.

When it comes to the referencing existing variables, you can always add directory at the end of the path command. You should keep in mind that modifying and adding environment variables in this particular way only sets the environment for your current session and any changes made will not be preserved for next sessions.

Chapter 3: How To Be Completely Anonymous Online Like The Pro's

Being hacker means breaking into the system, being individual who is modifying valuable information and sharing it with the world without certain authorization. Hacker gets into the system by the communication networks. Hacker essentially means computer programmer who can subvert any computer security. On the other side, there are hackers hacking with malicious purpose. These people are criminals, and they are illegally accessing computer systems. I mentioned before hackers stealing and entering into banks' and companies' computer security.

Hackers use their abilities and knowledge in computer science also good purposes as well. We are going to pay attention only to ethical and moral hacking. On the other hand, there is no surprise; hackers are disreputable. We heard about many cases in the past about stealing information which resulted in many accounts being compromised and many unauthorized transfers happen. Many banks and companies were targets and hit with the hacking attack. These attacks cost huge amount of money to both banks and companies, great amount of lost resources spent on investigation, more than stolen amount.

Hackers with malicious purposes besides stealing from banks and companies, usually steal peoples' personal information, online accounts especially social accounts and other personal files and data. When it comes to the ethical and moral hacking, you should keep in mind that you are always at risk to get caught. In this chapter, we are going to see how to be completely anonymous like a professional. Of course, keep in mind only ethical and moral hacking for good purposes is desirable hacking and any other purpose will not be discussed.

There are certain strategies and techniques how to hack like a professional and not get caught. Hackers like to get through many obstacles and penetrate into the computer system, and best way to do that is to be completely anonymous. Any other way is suspicious and may be dangerous. There are many restrictions while entering the computer system. An essential thing is being anonymous online and protecting your work. Hackers have to stay anonymous and not get traced by many tricks like using stronger passwords or using two-factor authentication.

How not to be caught and stay anonymous?

1.   When it comes to the tips of being completely anonymous while hacking, the most important thing you can do is

try not use windows operating system. For the perfect hacking environment, you will need unix operating system which is perfect for hacking job. Getting Linux operating system and computer will be money good spent. Windows operating system is not good for hacking due to many holes that can be traced easily. These windows holes in the security may be deciding factor in spyware infecting and compromising your anonymity. You should definitely use other operating system security hardened system.

2.   The second thing you should pay attention is to avoid connecting to the internet directly. You can easily be tracked through your IP address. So if you want to avoid this, you should use VPN services which stand for virtual private network. The virtual private

network allows users to share and receive files and data while online through public networks like the internet. While you are online using virtual private network, you are connected as if your computer is directly connected to the private network. All of the applications you are running through a virtual private network can benefit in functionality and security. With a virtual private network, you are going to be able to surf the internet with great security and lower risk of being caught.

How does VPN help you stay anonymous?

In order to be connected to the virtual private network, you will need to connect to the proxy servers which have purpose of protecting your identity and location as well. However many sites on the internet are blocking access to the virtual private network technology in order to prevent unauthorized entering and wandering.

VPN is essentially point to point connection which is using other connections and virtual tunneling protocols. Many benefits are provided by using a virtual private network for a wide-area network.

When it comes to the hacking, VPN will let you create private tunnel, anyone who is trying to trace your IP address will only see the address of the virtual private network server, and you can choose any address in the world.

Which VPN to use?

When it comes to the virtual private network services, there are plenty of options. Some of the best software for secure and private browsing the internet are ExpressVPN, NordVPN, PureVPN and all of these are free to download. You should keep in mind before downloading VPN software that not all of these are created equal. Some of the VPN software may offer you top notch services while others can play fast with your files and data. Before buying and downloading any of the VPN software keep this in mind.

3.   TOR is network full of nodes which are routing your traffic. Directions of the nodes are behind and in front. Your direction onto normal internet connections is known as exit point. The most secure and the best way is to combine both virtual private network and TOR. In order to be anonymous while being connected to the internet, you should download free TOR software. TORsoftware is going to protect your personal data from network surveillance and help you defend against trafficking analysis. These types of network surveillance threaten all of your personal privacy and work against your freedom. TOR software will protect and secure

your internet connection and prevent other people from seeing sites you are visiting. The most important thing is that TOR software is completely free for downloading.

4. Another one crucial thing when it comes to the hacking is email address. You should never use your email address while hacking. Instead of using your real email address, you should use one from the anonymous email service. Anonymous email service is letting their users send and receive emails from someone without any trace especially if you already have TOR software and virtual private network. When you go online every site is background checking your activities like google which is expecting you to share some of your personal information like email address or number.

Which email service software to get?

In order to set completely anonymous email address that can't be traced and without a connection to any server I recommend you download the software Hushmail's. Hushmail's is software very easy to use without any advertising, but it comes with the price, and on the other hand there is free version offering 25 MB of storage. If you don't want to pay extra money for the software, another great anonymous email service is software Guerilla Mail. Messages received in this mail are only temporary and will be available only for an hour.

Great way to stay anonymous and hide your email existence is website Mailinator, free and disposable. Whenever someone asks you for the email, you just make one up and sign into the Mailinator account and check received mail without leaving any traces. With the combination of the anonymous email service, TOR software and accessing connection through the virtual private network you are almost invisible to the others. By doing this, you protected your personal information and defended from the third party sites which are tracking your IP address and location every time you go online.

5.   It may seem obvious, but you should never use Google while hacking. Google is constantly tracking sites that you are visiting and all of your online activities. Google is the most useful search engine, and there is certain way for you to use it without revealing your identity and personal information. You should use some of the services for preventing Google storing your IP address, records of your searches and cookies. I recommend you to use services such as

StartPage or DuckDuck go which will prevent google from remembering your online searches and history of your online activity. You will be able to search through the google without compromising your identity.

6. Last but not least thing you should keep in mind is using public wireless connection. There is huge issue when it comes to the using public WiFi. The problem is that your computer has unique address, which is going to be recorded by the router of any public location. So if your address is tracked down by the router, it will lead to your location and device. The second problem with using public Wifi is common hacking attacks. Attacking public Wifi is known as man-in-the-middle, and it will compromise your anonymity. In that case, other hacker connected to the same

network connection as you will be able to track you down. These are basic tips and precautions when it comes to the anonymity while going online and staying safe and protected while hacking.

Chapter 4: How To Setup NMAP

We are already halfway; now you are familiar with the basics when it comes to the hacking. We already discussed Linux Terminal and tips and precautions for you to stay completely anonymous and protect your identity while hacking. The next thing of great importance is setting up NMAP which stand for network mapper. Network Mapper is the type of security scanner which is used in order to discover any hosts and service on the devices. A computer network is filled with anonymous hosts and services, and NMAP is tracking and discovering them and putting them together by building the certain map of network. Hence the name network mapper. In order to do this network mapper is sending special packets to the different hosts which are targets in this case and then NMAP analyzes the responses from the hosts.

Network mapping software provides many great utilities such as host discovery, operating system detection, and vulnerability detection. These are all great features for probing computer network. Besides these basic features, NMAP provides many other advanced features. Network mapper tool is constantly being developed and refined by the computer science community. Firstly it started as Linux utility, but later expanding to the other platforms such as Solaris, Windows, and IRIX. Among the IT community, NMAP utility for Linux is the most popular today and closely followed by operating system Windows.

There is no surprise that network mapper is great tool when it comes to the hacking. You should keep in mind that computer network is filled with the great number of hosts and services and network mapping is a great way to discover them all. Some of the features that network mapper provides are port scanning, determining operating system, scriptable interaction with the hosts and detection of the version meaning interrogating network services. Network mapper is used when it comes to the generating traffic to the target, finding any vulnerabilities, auditing security of your computer and analyzing open ports and preparing for auditing.

Now we should see how to setup network mapper scanning. It may sound terrifying, but it is quite easy to do, and often NMAP can be installed just by doing one command. As I said, NMAP could work on many different platforms provided with both source code compilation and installation methods.

➤ The first logical step for you is to check if you already have network mapper installed. Many platforms already have NMAP tool installed such as Linux and BSD. To find out if you already have NMAP, you should open terminal window and execute command NMAP, and if NMAP already exists, you will see that in the output. On the other hand, if you don't have NMAP installed you will see error message. In any case, you should consider having the latest version of network mapper and upgrading it.

NMAP is running from shell prompt. This is letting users to quickly execute the commands without wandering around bunch of configuration scripts and option fields. It may be intimidating for the beginners the fact that NMAP tools have a great number of command-line options even though some of them are ignored by many users such as commands for debugging. Interpreting and executing any outcome will be easy once you figure out how the command-line works and how to pick among command-line options,

➤ In case you don't have NMAP already installed, you should download one from the internet. Nmap.Org is right place for downloading hence it is official source for downloading. You can download from the Nmap.Org both source codes and binaries. Source codes will come in the shape of compressed tar files and binaries are available for many platforms including Linux and Windows.

➤ After you downloaded source codes and binaries from the Nmap.Org, you may be intimidated by the verifying the integrity of the maps downloaded. Many of the popular packages of the maps such as OpenSSH, Libpcap or Fragrouter may be easily infected with the great number of malicious trojans. The Same thing can happen to the software distribution sites such as SourceForge and Free Software Foundation. You should be careful not to download infected files.

➤ When it comes to the verifying NMAP tools, you should consult the PGP signatures that come together with the NMAP version you downloaded. When you download NMAP, you will get both PGP signatures and cryptographic hashes. You can find both in the NMAP signatures directory. The most secure way of verification of the NMAP is PSG signatures which came with the tool. Of course, you will need NMAP special signing key because NMAP versions are signed with these special keys. In order to get one visit on of the popular key servers. Once you get the special signing key, you will import it through the command, and you are only doing this once. By doing this, you are verifying all of your future releases.

It is easy when it comes to the verification with the proper signature key, and it takes single command. Besides signature keys, there are other options for verifying the NMAP like MD5 and SHA1 hashes if you are more into casual validation. But be careful, hashes from third party sites may easily be infected and corrupted. Once you verify NMAP, you can build the network of the host sand servers from the source code.

Chapter 5: Which Tools The Hackers Use To Crack Passwords

You already know who is a hacker. Hackers are using their knowledge and abilities to break into the system, to access the information and modify and create something completely new. Now it is time to see which tools the hackers use in order to break into system and to crack passwords. The first and most important thing is as I mentioned before is operating system Linux which will give you complete power when it comes to using hacking tools of any kind.

There are many different types of tools for hacking, depending on the purpose and knowledge of the users. Keep in mind what type of the hacking and for which purpose you are going to do. Depending on your personal interest you may need tools for firewalls, intrusion detection systems, root kit detectors, packet crafting tools, wireless hacking or vulnerability exploitation tools. All of these tools come bundled with Linux, so I recommend Linux appropriate toolbox.

I already mentioned network mapper as a very useful hacking tool for discovering and mapping network hosts. When it comes to the cracking password, there is a great number of tools and software of great importance for the hackers.

There are many ways of cracking password depending on the tool used.

Most common ways include cracking passwords:

- with the help of brute forcing
- by using dictionary attacks cracking encrypted passwords
- with the hashes cracking windows passwords

- by analyzing wireless packets cracking of WEP or WPA passwords
- by identifying different kinds of injections and scripts and discovering hidden scripts and resources.

Here is the list of cracking password tools I would recommend.

1. Aircrack-ng:

Aircrack-ng is really powerful cracking tool which includes analysis tool, detectors, and WPA crackers. Among these utilities, it also includes a great number of analysis tools for wireless LAN. It is working for cracking passwords with a wireless network interface. The wireless network interface has the controller which drivers support raw mode of monitoring and can take up a great traffic. The most important thing is that this tool is completely free to download and can work on any platforms including OSX, OpenBSD, and

Linux. This tool is perfect for cracking password due to its work in the field of the WiFi security. This tool focuses on the monitoring and capturing packets and exporting it to files which will be processed by the third party tools.

2. Crowbar

This is the second great tool for cracking password used by many hackers. Crowbar is one of the most powerful brute force cracking tools. When you are using Crowbar, you have opportunity to be in the control of things submitted to web servers. Crowbar is not identifying positive responses, but it is comparing content of the responses with the baseline. Crowbar is completely free for downloading and works only with Linux operating system. Crowbar is powerful tool when it comes to the supporting role and is used during penetration tests.

3.   John The Ripper

It is s the most popular password cracking tool. It is really powerful and highly effective when it comes to the cracking, and that is why John The Ripper is the part of the huge family of hacking tools Rapid7.In the field of the cryptographic system, hackers are trying to find any vulnerabilities in the security network. Cracking password means recovering password from the data previously stored by the computer system or network. One of the most popular ways of cracking a password is known as brute-force attack in which computer simply guesses and hash the passwords. If you want to be real professional in the hacking world, you should get to know more about cryptographic science. John The Ripper can be downloaded for free online, and there is also pro version which you can buy. For cracking a password, this commercial version will be enough providing you great performance and speed.

Originally John The Ripper was developed only for Unix-like operating systems, but today it can work on different platforms. This tool is the best option when it comes to the only cracking passwords.

4.   Medusa

I can't discuss hacking tools and not to mention another great hacking tool Medusa. Medusa is also brute force tool providing users with excellent performance. The biggest advantage of this tools is thread-based testing allowing you to fight against multiple hosts and users. Medusa is developed in modular design, with great features like flexible user input and it is completely free to download. Medusa is running on Linux and MAC OS X operating systems. This tool can perform attacks with great speed against a large number of protocols such as HTTP, telnet, and databases.

Besides these tools for cracking a password, I

warmly recommend RainbowCrack, SolarWinds and THC Hydra.

Chapter 6: TOR And The DarkNet

I already mentioned TOR and some of its features which are very powerful software when it comes to the staying anonymous while hacking and being online. TOR is software that enables users anonymous communication by directing traffic on the internet through worldwide and free networks which are consisting of more thousands of relays all over the world. TOR is concealing your location from anyone online including all kinds of network surveillance and analysis of network traffic. By using TOR, you are making it harder for the internet activity to be traced back to you while you are online. You are preventing from being traced and hiding all of your instant messages, online posts and any visit to the web sites. TOR is originally developed in order to protect personal information, to give more freedom to the users and protect them while being online.

TOR is developed by encryption of the communication stack, nested like layers of the onion. It is working by encrypting a huge number of files including IP addresses multiple times and sending it to the virtual circuit. After the encryption is done and the innermost part of the encryption is sent to the final destination without revealing and knowing the source of the IP address. This is possible due to routing in the communication, and the IP address is more concealing by the hop in the TOR circuit. This method eliminates any way of communication peers being traced back to the user. Since network surveillance relies upon determining and discovering users destination and source, by using TOR software you will prevent revealing your identity and location to the network surveillance and be free from traffic analysis.

Beside Tor software the other important compound when it comes to the hacking world is DarkNet. DarkNet is special type of network, overlay networking allowing its users to access it only with special software and configuration. To enter into DarkNet network, you will also need specific authorization. DarkNet network is usually using non-standards protocols of communication and specific ports for accessing. There are two types of DarkNet networks. First one is friend –to-friend and privacy networks. A friend-to-friend network is usually used for file sharing, and TOR is the second one used as strictly privacy network.

You shouldn't mix DarkNet with the deep web. The deep web is the term referring to the all hidden parts of the internet which can't be accessed by any search engine such as Google and Yahoo. Some of the experts believe that content of the deep web is much bigger than the surface web. In fact, the deep web doesn't contain anything sinister but contain large databases and libraries which can be accessed only by members. Some of the search engines of deep web are FreeNet and TorSearch. DarkNet is just small part of the much bigger is known as for anonymous internet.

When you are surfing through DarkNet, both web surfers and publishers are completely anonymous. You will achieve anonymous communication using TOR software. When you are connected to the regular internet network, your computer accesses host server of the site you are visiting, but with the TOR software that link is broken. Your communication will be registered on the network, but TOR will prevent transport mediums from knowing who is doing communication. TOR as a part of DarkNet utility is perfect for anonymous communication and online freedom, running on most operating systems.

The DarkNet was originally developed for the military and government, and today they are mostly using the benefits of the DarkNet. Regular internet connection and network can easily discover your location, and this is the main reason for using DarkNet. It is also popular among journalists, politicians, activists and revolutionaries. Accessing the hidden contents of the internet is really easy. Like I said before, installing TOR browser will let you enter the DarkNet. Besides Tor, you can install TheFreeNet project for accessing hidden contents on the internet and allows you in creating private networks, unlike TOR. There is another privacy network I2P which stands for the invisible internet project.

For the absolute anonymity, you should use TOR or any other privacy network together with VPN and nobody will be able to see your online activities. There is no wonder why these software for privacy are really popular today. You are never too protected. You should always keep in mind that all of the search engines you are using are tracking and remembering all of your activities while being connected to the network. Surfing through the DarkNet with TOR software you are making great steps in staying anonymous and protecting your personal information.

Chapter 7: How You Can Use Multiple Tools To Gather Information With Wireless Hacking

While cracking wireless networks, hackers are attacking and defeating devices responsible for security of the network. WLANs is wireless local-area network known as WiFi. WLANs are extremely vulnerable due to the security holes. Wireless hacking is direct attract and intrusion, and there are two main problems when it comes to the wireless security. The first problem is due to the weak configuration and secondly is due to weak encryption.

You should keep in mind that hacking attack is hard job, step by step procedure. Hackers are using many techniques and strategies in order to get full access. You will need to know many combinations and methods in order to break into the security through security holes. Every wireless network is potential hole as well as wired network. Real hackers must rely on their knowledge in computer science, physical skills, social engineering and any other work that involves interaction between people.

When it comes to the wireless hacking, there are plenty of options available. Here is the list of options:

1.   **Aircrack:** It is not only one of the most powerful tools; it is also one of the most popular ones for wireless hacking. Aircrack is developed for using the best algorithms in order to recover passwords by discovering and tracking down packets. Once the packet is captured Aircrack will try to recover the password. In order to attack with greater speed, it implements standard FMS attack with better optimization. There are great online video tutorials how to use Aircrack tool, and it is running on the

Linux operating system. If you are using Aircrack on the Linux, it will require more knowledge of Linux.

2. **Airsnort:** It is another great and powerful tool for wireless hacking besides Aircrack. Airsnort is a powerful tool used for decrypting any WEP wireless network encryption. The best thing is that Airsnort is completely free to download and is running both on Linux and Windows operating systems. Airsnort works in the way of monitoring computing keys and transmissions when it has enough packets previously received. Due to its simple use, this tool is perfect for beginners.

3. **Kismet:** It is another great tool used by a great number of people for wireless hacking. This one is the wireless network sniffer. Kismet is working with any

wireless card and supports rfmon mode as well. Kismet is working by collecting and receiving packets passively and identifying hidden networks. You can download it for free, and it is available for many platforms including Linux, OSX, and BSD.

4.   **NetStumbler**: It is wireless hacking tool used worldwide by a huge number of people. NetStumbler is running only on the Windows operating system and can be downloaded for free. There is also mini version of NetStumbler available called MiniStumbler. This tool is mainly developed for war driving and discovering unauthorized access points. There is great disadvantage when it comes to this tool. It can easily detect by the most intrusion systems which are available today. Besides this, the tool is working poorly running on the64bit

Windows operating system. NetStumbler is working by actively collecting useful information from the network.

5. **inSSIDer:** It is one great and popular wireless scanner for Windows operating system. This tool was originally free to download but became premium, so you will have to pay in order to get inSSIDer tool. Among many tasks that this tool can perform the most important are finding open wireless access points and saving logs from by the GPS.

6. **WireShark:** It is really powerful tool used as network analyzer. With WireShark, you will be able to see what is happening in your personal network. With this tool, you can easily live capture and analyze any packets. You can check a large number of data fast and at micro-

mode. It is working on many platforms including Solaris, Windows, FreeBSD, Linux and many other. In order to use WireShark, you have to be familiar with network protocols.

7.   **coWPAtty:** It is a perfect tool when it comes to the automated dictionary attacking. It is running only on the Linux operating system. With the command line interface containing a word lists with the passwords for executing the attack. This tool is perfect for the beginners, but disadvantage is that tool is slow in the process. Dictionary is used for cracking passwords, cracking the each word that is contained in the dictionary.

8.   **Airjack:** It is wireless cracking tool with wide range of people using it. Airjack is running as packet injection tool, hence

the name Airjack. This tool is making network go down by injecting packets.

Other than the tools, I mentioned here, and I also recommend you other tools such as WepAttack, OmniPeek, and CloudCracker.

Chapter 8: How To Keep Yourself Safe From Being Hacked

In this last chapter, we should discuss how to stay safe and not get hacked. Hackers can break into your personal computer network if you are not careful. They can steal your personal information. You should be careful when it comes to your digital life and take some precautions before going online and compromising yourself to the world. You should keep in mind that professional hackers can have bad purposes, can steal your bank accounts, your personal emails, and social media accounts as well. Keeping yourself from being hacked is of great importance for safe and protected digital life.

➤ **Be Careful about what you Share Online**

First and the most important thing is to be careful what you share online. Posting online info which is usually asked as security questions are not good idea. All of this information can be used by hackers to break into your personal accounts. Hackers are able to steal millions of password and personal files, causing blackouts. These tips are of great importance for not letting that happen to you.

➤ **Setting Strong and Unique Passwords**

You should always use strong and unique password. By adding extra level of protection known as two-factor authentication, you are making yourself more protected. By enabling two-factor, you are going to need something more besides password to log into your account. Often it is numerical code which is sent to your cellphone.

➤ Download a Password Manager Tool

Before going online, I recommend you to download a password manager tool, which is going to save all of your passwords. I recommend you to download Dashlane or 1Password.

➤ Use LittleSnitch

I previously mentioned you should use virtual private network that will prevent intruders from entering into your personal network by routing the internet traffic. Another great software for staying safe while being connected to the network is LittleSnitch which monitors all of your outgoing connections. It will alert you whenever computer is trying to send files to the unknown server. Your laptop should be using full disk encryption, if not you should turn it on.

➤ Don't Underestimate the Importance of Antivirus Programs

You should keep in mind the importance of antivirus programs. And yes, it is true that antivirus are basically full of security holes, but still having an antivirus program installed is a good idea for staying protected from trojans. Besides using antiviruses, I recommend using simple security plugins such a sad blockers.

➤ Stop Using Flash

If you are using flash, you should know that flash is the most insecure software with a great number of security holes perfect for hackers.

➤ Backup Your Files Regularly

Finally, yet importantly, the last

recommendation is to back up your files regularly. You should back up your files usually when you are disconnected from the network. You should use external hard disk in case you get ransom ware.

You should never underestimate potential danger and threat. Hackers are always lurking new victims, take these precautions for staying safe and protected while being online. These tips can be life changing when it comes to the digital life and online freedom.

Conclusion

Here we are at the end of the road. We discussed basics when it comes to the hacking with step by step guides. I think now you are ready to do some real hacking job. Now you are familiar with tools of great importance for hacking, using Linux Terminal is no foreign to you, you are able to crack some serious wireless network connections and be protected while wandering through the internet. Like I said before you should keep in mind that hacker job is going to take many sacrifices and it will cost you many sleepless nights. I don't want to discourage you, and you just need to be prepared in every possible way.

Learning and expanding your limits is the most essential when it comes to the hacking. Knowledge will get you on the right path and secure you successful job. Now you have considerable amount of knowledge in hacking to start with real cracking and hacking. You know there is enormous amount of knowledge out there on the computers, and there is no possible way for single person to access it all and learn everything. You will eventually figure out in which field of computer science are you interested the most. Maybe you are mostly interested in software development or computer security, in both cases, you will need to know basics in order to improve your skills and upgrade your knowledge.

Hacking is knowing what is going on inside the network and computer and understanding all of the processes happening inside the devices. By knowing what is going on inside the computer and breaking into the system, you will be able to modify information you accessed and create something completely new. By accessing and breaking into huge databases and libraries, you will have all of the information you need. You will have the real power in your hands. And for the end, you should keep in mind that only ethical and moral hacking is for good purposes. You just need to dedicate your work towards ethical purposes.

In order to get the most out of this book we have included a FREE BONUS on the next page. This will help increase your understanding of Hacking and overall computer programming.

The Blueprint to Raspberry Pi 3

A Beginners Guide: Everything You Need to Know for Starting Your Own Projects

By: Cyber Punk Architects

Introduction

Thank you for downloading my book
*"Raspberry Pi: The Blueprint for Raspberry Pi
3: Everything You Need to Know for Starting
Your Own Projects"*. Recently the Raspberry Pi
has been receiving a ton of press coverage and
capturing the curiosity of people all around the
world, at least people who are technology
journalists and enthusiasts. As time has passed,
more and more people have heard of this
fascinating small single board computer
stamped with chips and connectors, but many
people aren't sure exactly what it is.

If you are one of those people who is intrigued
by the tastily named Raspberry Pi, this book is
for you. In this book, we are going to look at a
quick overview of what the Raspberry Pi is, and
then we are going to break down the
specifications and what they mean. Finally, we
are going to look at all the amazing projects the

Raspberry Pi can assist you with. Whether you are well-versed in technology or diving into it for the first time, this book is going to help you.

By the time, you are done reading this book, you are going to have the knowledge to use your Raspberry Pi with ease to do anything from watching a movie to playing games, and from creating a spreadsheet to learning how to program.

Chapter 1: Raspberry Pi – An Overview

The Raspberry Pi has many incredible features. The largest appeal of the Raspberry Pi computer is that it is a small size, and is also affordable. The Raspberry Pi can be used as a traditional computer by simply being plugged into a TV and a keyboard. Since 2012, there have been many models of the Raspberry Pi released to the public, each with their own improvements and changes.

Approximately the size of a credit card and available for as little as $5USD, the intended purpose of the Raspberry Pi was to bring affordable computer options to everyone. Below, we are going to take a brief look at the different models of Raspberry Pi.

Raspberry Pi 1 Model A – This was the original model of the Raspberry Pi. Released in

February 2012. This was followed up late by the Raspberry Pi 1 Model A Plus which was released in November 2014, which featured a larger hard drive and a lower price point.

Raspberry Pi 1 Model B– The Generation 1 and 1 Plus of the Model B Raspberry Pi were released in April 2012 and July 2014 respectively. The 1 Plus had a lower price point than the original Model B and featured a microSD slot instead of the standard SD slot.

Raspberry Pi Zero – This was a smaller model that was released in November 2015. The size of the Zero was smaller and it had a reduced input and output. This is the cheapest model of Raspberry Pi that is currently available for purchase. The original Zero did not include video input. However, a second version released in May 2016 included video input options similar to other models.

Raspberry Pi 2 – This model included more ram than any of the previous models and was released in February 2015. This model is at the high end of all Raspberry Pi products and can be found for just $35USD.

Raspberry Pi 3 Model B – This is the newest model of Raspberry Pi. Released in February 2016, the Raspberry Pi 3, Model B is bundled with the additions including onboard Wi-Fi, Bluetooth, and USB boot capabilities. We will cover more on this later in this book.

There are a few things that are common among all the versions of Raspberry Pi. This includes the Broadcom system on a chip, which features a CPU (Central Processing System) that is compatible with ARM, as well as on-chip GPU (Graphics Processing Unit).

The boards all have between one and four USB slots, as well as an HDMI slot, composite video output and a 3.5 mm phone jack for audio capabilities.

The creators of Raspberry Pi provide *Raspbian*, which is a Debian-based Linux distribution for download. It also provides third party *Ubuntu*, *Windows 10* IOT Core, RISC OS, and other specialized media center distributions. While the Raspberry Pi supports many programming languages, it promotes Python and Scratch as its main programming language. You also have the option of open source or closed source firmware, although the default firmware is closed source.

Chapter 2: Raspberry Pi 3 – Model B Hardware Specifications

There have been several evolutions in the hardware that the Raspberry Pi offers. In this chapter, we are going to focus on the Raspberry Pi 3 – Model B specifically.

For the purpose of keeping this book easy to read for those of you who aren't as familiar with the technological jargon, while keeping it interesting for those of you who don't need as in depth of an explanation, this chapter is going to be broken down into sections that allow you to skim through and find the information you are looking for without having to read every explanation.

Wireless Radio – Broadcom BCM43438

This wireless radio has been expertly built directly into the board to keep the cost of the

Raspberry Pi down. It is also so small; you are going to be able to see the markings through a microscope or magnifying glass. The Broadcom BCM43438 chip gives the Raspberry Pi 2.4 GHZ 802.11n wireless LAN, Bluetooth Low Energy, and Bluetooth 4.1 Classic radio support. This is what is going to allow you to connect your Raspberry Pi to the internet, both through a wired connection as well as through a wireless connection.

SoC – Broadcom BCM2837

This SoC (System on Chip) has been built specifically for the Raspberry Pi 3 – Model B. This SoC features four high-performance ARM Cortex-A53 processing cores which run at 1.2GHz and have 32kB level one and 512kB level two memory. It also has a Video Core IV graphics processor and is also linked to the one gigabyte LPDDR2 memory module that is located on the rear of the board.

GPIO – 40-Pin Header, Populated

The GPIO (General Purpose Input Output) header is the same on this Raspberry Pi as it has been going back through most of the Raspberry Pi models. This means that any existing GPIO hardware is going to work with the Raspberry Pi 3 – Model B without any further modifications needed. The only change that has been made to this part of the Raspberry Pi is a change to which UART is exposed on the pins. However, this doesn't affect usage as the operating system internally handles it.

USB Chip – SMSC LAN9514

This is another part of the Raspberry Pi that hasn't changed from the Raspberry Pi 2. The SMSC LAN9514 adds 10/100 Ethernet connectivity as well as four USB channels to the board. The chip connects to the SoC through a single USB channel, acting as a USB to Ethernet adaptor as well as a USB hub.

To sum up all the information above:

SoC: Broadcom BCM2837

CPU: 4× ARM Cortex-A53, 1.2GHz

GPU: Broadcom VideoCore IV

RAM: 1GB LPDDR2 (900 MHz)

Networking: 10/100 Ethernet, 2.4GHz 802.11n wireless

Bluetooth: Bluetooth 4.1 Classic, Bluetooth Low Energy

Storage: microSD

GPIO: 40-pin header, populated

Ports: HDMI, 3.5mm analog audio-video jack, 4× USB 2.0, Ethernet, Camera Serial Interface (CSI), Display Serial Interface (DSI)

Now that we are all familiar with the hardware that is inside the Raspberry Pi 3 – Model B, we are going to have a look at the software.

Chapter 3: Raspberry Pi 3 – Software Specifications

One of the neat things about the Raspberry Pi 3 – Model B is that you can run almost any software on it. While it primarily uses *Raspbian*, which is a Debian-based Linux operating system, you are not limited to using this. In this chapter, we are going to run through all the different operating systems, driver APIs, firmware and other third party application software that will be accessible to you for use on the Raspberry Pi 3 – Model B.

Operating Systems

On the official Raspberry Pi website, you will have access to Ubuntu Mate, Snappy Ubuntu Core, Windows 10 IoT Core, and RISC OS, as well as specialized distributions for the Kodi media center and classroom management.

Below we are going to cover every operating systemthat can be used, categorized by those that are Linux based and those that not Linux based.

Linux Based Operating Systems:

Alpine Linux – This is a Linux distribution that is based on *musl* and *BusyBox*. It has been primarily designed for those power users who require more security, simplicity, and resource efficiency.

Android Things – This is an embedded version of the Android operating system that is designed for IoT device development.

Ark OS – This operating system has been designed for website and email self-hosting.

CentOS – This is a newer operating system that is only available for Raspberry Pi 2 and newer.

Diet Pi – This operating system includes a diverse range of servers that are ideal for media, Minecraft, VPN, and much more.

Fedora 25 – This is another newer operating system that is only available for the newer Raspberry Pi models.

Gentoo – This operating system is ideal for users who want full control of the software that they use on their Raspberry Pi 3.

Instant WebKiosk – This operating system is ideal for users who are looking for digital signage purposes such as web and media views.

Kali Linux – This operating system is a Debianderived distro that has been designed for digital forensics and penetration testing.

Kano OS – This operating system is one that you can build and customize to be exactly what you want it to be for you. Completely free, this is a great choice if you want to have full control over your operating system.

MinePeon – This operating system has been designed to be dedicated to mining cryptocurrency.

Moebius – This is another operating system that is based on Debian. This operating system is a light ARM HF distribution that uses Raspbian repository but fits onto a 128 MB SD card. This operating system only offers minimal services and has had its memory use optimized to keep it small.

NARD SDK – This is a software development kids that is intended for industrial embedded systems.

OpenSUSE – This is another operating system that gives you full control over creating the code for your system.

OpenWrt – This operating system is primarily used to route network traffic on embedded devices.

Pardus ARM – This operating system is another option for a Debian derived system. This is the light version of the Pardus operating system that is popular with the Turkish Government.

Pidora – This is a Fedora Remix that has been optimized for use on the Raspberry Pi.

ROKOS – This operating system is another

Rasbian based option that is integrated for use with Bitcoin and OKCashcryptocurrencies.

Tingbot OS – This operating system has been designed to be used primarily with the Tingbot add-on as well as running Tide applications. This operating system is also based on the Raspbian operating system.

Tiny Core Linux – This operating system is designed to run primarily in RAM. It is a minimal Linux operating system where the primary focus is to provide a base system using BusyBox and FLTK.

Void Linux – This operating system is a rolling release Linux distribution that has been designed and implemented from scratch. Void Linux provides images based on musl or glibc.

WTware for Raspberry Pi – This is a free operating system that is used for the creation of Windows thin client.

Xbian – This operating system uses the Kodi open source digital media center.

Not Linux Based Operating Systems:

Genode OS Framework – This operating system is a toolkit that is used to build highly secure special purpose operating systems. This is not the operating system that would be best for those who are just starting out, however, if you have a lot of experience with coding, this is a good choice.

HelenOS – This operating system is a portable multi-server that is microkernel-based.

NetBSD – This operating system is another that will allow you to create the coding and use your Raspberry Pi 3 – Model B however, you decide.

Plan 9 – This is an open source operating system that is similar to Unix. It was originally developed at Bell Labs as a research operating system. When you are using Plan 9, everything is treated as a file regardless of whether it is a local or network resource.

Xv6 – This is a modern version of the Sixth Edition Unix operating system that has been re-implemented for teaching purposes. It is easily ported to the Raspberry Pi from MIT xv6 which can be booted from NOOBS (New Out of Box Software).

Media Center Operating Systems – If you are looking for operating systems that are going to run your Raspberry Pi 3 – Model B as a media center your best options are OSMC, OpenELEC, LibreELEC, XBIAN, and Rasplex.

Audio Operating Systems – If you want to use your Raspberry Pi 3 – Model B for audio, the best operating systems are going to include Volumio, Pimusicbox, Runeaudio, and moOdeaudio.

Retrogaming Operating Systems – If you want to use your Raspberry Pi 3 – Model B to play retro games, the ideal operating systems include Retropie, Recalbox, Happi Game Centre, Lakka, ChameleonPi, and Piplay.

Driver APIs

Raspberry Pi 3 – Model B has the capability to use a VideoCore IV GPU through a binary blob.

The binary blob is loaded into the GPU when it is booted from the SD card. Much of the driver work was originally done using the closed source GPU code, although there are software applications such as OpenMAX, OpenGL ES, or OpenVG which can be used to call an open course driver in the VideoCore IV GPU driver code.

Firmware

The official firmware of the Raspberry Pi 3 – Model B is a closed course binary blob that is freely redistributable. There is also open source firmware that is available minimally.

Third Party Application Software

As well as the operating systems that we covered in this chapter, there are many options for other software that can be put onto your Raspberry Pi 3 – Model B from third parties. In this section, we are going to briefly look at some of the more popular third party applications.

Mathematica – Raspbian includes a full installation of this software for free. This allows programs to be run from either a command line interface or from a notebook interface. Some of the language functions allow for accessing connected devices.

Minecraft – In February 2013, a version of Minecraft was released for Raspberry Pi that allows you to modify the game world with code. This is the only official version of Minecraft that allows this.

RealVNC – RealVNC's remote access server and viewer software are included with the Raspbian operating system. This includes the new capture technology which allows content to be directly rendered as well as non-X11 applications to be viewed and controlled remotely.

UserGate Web Filter – In 2013, Entensys, a

security vendor based in Florida, announced they would be porting Usergate Web Filter to the Raspberry Pi Platform.

Software Development

In addition to the addition applications listed above, there are programs available that can help you learn more about developing software. Learning how to develop software will help you be able to use the Raspberry Pi 3 – Model B to its fullest potential.

AlgolD – This is a program that is ideal for teaching programming to children as well as beginners in the programming world.

Julia – This is a programming language that is both interactive and able to be used across multiple platforms. IDE's for Julia are also available including June and JuliaBerry, which is a Pi specific repository.

Scratch – This teaching tool uses visual blocks that stack to teach IDE. MIT's Life Long

Kindergarten group originally developed this. The version that was created for Pi is heavily optimized for the limited computing resources that are available and work well with the Squeak Smalltalk system.

Now that you are aware of the software options that are available for you to use with your Raspberry Pi 3 – Model B, we are going to explore how you can go about configuring your Raspberry Pi to do what you want it to do.

Chapter 4: Configuring Raspberry Pi

Once you have your Raspberry Pi 3 – Model B in your possession, you are going to want to get it set up and ready to use. The good news is that setting it up is easy and takes less than thirty minutes. That means that before you know it, you are going to be ready to start doing some awesome stuff with your new piece of technology!

Before You Start

Before you get started, there are a few supplies you are going to need on hand in addition to the Raspberry Pi to get through the set-up process and move on to amazing projects.

HDMI television or monitor – You are going to need to connect your Raspberry Pi to a display which means that you need some sort of HDMI enabled screen. You don't need to use a full-sized monitor for your Raspberry Pi, and there are compact options on the market. There are also ways around using a monitor at all, which we will discuss later in this chapter.

USB keyboard and mouse – In order to be able to control your Raspberry Pi 3 – Model B, you are going to need to have a keyboard and mouse. Any USB keyboard and mouse will work for this.

8GB MicroSD card and card reader – Instead of using a hard drive, Raspberry Pi's operating system is installed with a MicroSD card. You are going to want at least 8Gb for this. Your computer might have a card reader. If it does not, all you are going to need is a cheap one,.Card readers can often be found for under $10 USD.

Power Supply – The Raspberry Pi 3 – Model B is powered by a micro USB, similar to the one you likely use for your cell phone. Since the Pi 3 – Model B has four USB ports, the best power supply is one that can provide at least 2.5A of power.

Step One – Install Raspbian Onto Your MicroSD Card with NOOBs

The first thing you are going to have to do before you can use your new Raspberry Pi 3 – Model B is to put Raspbian onto your MicroSD card. To do this, you first need to download the operating system on another computer and transfer it to your SD card. There are two ways you can do this. First, you can install Raspian manually. This required you to either know the command line, or external software. The second option, which is much simpler requires that you download and install NOOBs Since this is the easier option, this is the option we are going to review in this chapter.

1 – Put your SD card into your computer or SD card reader.

2 – Download NOOBs. Choose the option of

"offline and network install." This option will include Raspbian in the download itself.

3 – You may need to format your SD card as FAT. If so, download the SD Association's Formatting Tool which can be found at sdcard.org. Simply set the "Format Size Adjustment" to "on" in the options menu, and your SD card will be formatted.

4 – Extract the Zip file. Once the extraction is complete, copy the entire folder contents to your SD card. Once the copy is complete, you can eject your SD card and insert it into your Raspberry Pi 3 – Model B.

Step Two – Hook Up Your Raspberry Pi

The next step is to connect your devices to your Raspberry Pi 3 – Model B. Doing this is very easy, since all you need to do is plug stuff into the USB ports. However, it is important to do this is in the order listed below to ensure that all of your devices are recognized when you boot your Raspberry Pi up.

1 – Connect your monitor to your Raspberry Pi

2 – Connect your USB mouse and keyboard

3 – If you are using an Ethernet cable for your router, connect it now.

4 – Connect your power adapter. Since your Raspberry Pi 3 – Model B doesn't have a power switch, as soon as you connect the power source it is going to turn on.

Step Three – Set Up Raspbian

When you first boot up NOOBs, it is going to be busy for a couple of minutes formatting the SD card and setting things up. Let it do what it needs to do. Eventually, there will be a screen that will come up asking you to install an operating system.

1 – At the bottom of the screen there is going to be a place where you can select your language and keyboard layout for your region.

2 – Check the box that is next to the Raspbian

option and click install.

NOOBs willthen run the installation process, which can take anywhere from ten to twenty minutes. Once it is complete, the Raspberry Pi will restart itself and then send you straight to the Raspbian desktop where you will have the ability to configure everything else.

Step Four – Configure Your Raspberry Pi 3 – Model B

Your Raspberry Pi is now mostly ready to go. In Raspbian you are going to see a start menu. In this start menu, you are going to be able to select applications, open a file browser, and execute other commands that you might expect to be able to do with an operating system. The first thing you should do is set up your Wi-Fi, as well as any Bluetooth devices you want to use, with your Raspberry Pi.

Connect to Your Wi-Fi Network

Connecting to Wi-Fi through your Raspbian is just as easy as any modern operating system you may be accustomed to working with.

1 – Click the network icon. It is located at the top right corner and looks like two computers.

2 – Select your Wi-Fi network name and enter your password.

That's it. You are now connected to your Wi-Fi network. You are only going to need to do this once, and it will work in both the command line and the graphical interface.

Connect Bluetooth Devices

If you want to use a Bluetooth enabled mouse or keyboard with your Raspberry Pi 3 – Model B, you are going to need to pair them. Depending on the device you are pairing, this process can vary a bit, but using the directions below, you shouldn't have any issues.

1 – Click on the Bluetooth icon that is in the upper right corner of your screen.

2 – Click the "Add Device" option

3 – Find the device that you want to pair your Raspberry Pi with and follow the directions that appear on the screen to pair them up.

Once you have followed the directions above, your Raspberry Pi 3 – Model B is ready for you to start playing around with. If something goes wrong and you end up somehow messing up the programming, you can also follow the above steps to reinstall Raspbian and start over.

Connect to Your Raspberry Pi Remotely

Occasionally you might find yourself in a position where you may want to access your Raspberry Pi remotely. Maybe you don't have access to a monitor, or you only have a laptop in the house. Whatever reason you may have for wanting to connect remotely, it's handy to know that there are options.

Connect to The Command Line Through SSH – You can use SSH from any computer to connect to the command line interface of yourRaspberry Pi. While this option won't allow you to access a graphic interface, you can run any type of command from the Terminal application, and it'll execute on the Raspberry Pi. This is especially useful if you are working on a project that doesn't require a screen.

Use VNC To Use Your Home Computer as A Remote Screen – If your project requires that you do have a graphical interface, VNC (virtual network computing) to obtain it. You will be able to see the Raspberry Pi's desktop in a window on your computer desktop, and you will be able to control it like you are using the Pi. This isn't the best option for the day to day use as it is slow, but in the event that you only need to get a few things established and don't want to necessarily have touse the keyboard and mouse, this is an easy way to do so.

Now that you know how to get your Raspberry

118

Pi 3 – Model B up and running, in the next chapter, we are going to look at some of the programmingassociated with your Raspberry Pi.

Chapter 5: Programming In Raspberry Pi

The original purpose of the Raspberry Pi was to be able to teach people about technology. In this chapter, we are going to learn some of the basics of the two programming languages that are included in Raspbian, which is the recommended distribution for the Pi.

Scratch

This is a great language for those who are learning the basics of programming. Scratch doesn't require you to get the text perfect. Instead, everything is done by dragging and dropping program blocks into your script. This also means that you aren't going to have to remember any of the commands. For this example, we are going create a simple drawing program that will allow us to use the arrow keys to trace lines on the screen.

The first thing you are going to have to do is open Scratch. You will find Scratch in the **Menu**, under **Programming**. Once you have opened Scratch, you will see a screen with blocks of code, a scripts area, a stage where you can see your project, as well as some toolbars.

Now that we have the program open, we are going to create the code that will let us move the cat sprite around the screen.

We are going to use three separate blocks, each of which will be executed when a key is pressed. First, press the yellow control button, which is located on the left side of the screen near the top. Drag and drop the option "**When Space Key Pressed**" into the scripts box. This is going to create a script that will run whenever the space key is pressed. Use the drop-down menu and change **Space** to **Right Arrow**. Click on the blue motion button that is located next to the yellow control button and drag **Move 8 Steps** under **Right Arrow** in the scripts window. This will allow you to move the cat forward by pressing the right arrow.

Now that you have done that, create similar scripts that turn clockwise when the down key is pressed, and counter clockwise when the up key is pressed. Once you have finished that, we will be able to move around. However, we will need to add a block that will allow us to draw. Since we don't want to draw all the time, we will use Scratch's **pen up** and **pen down** actions. When the pen is down, the cat will leave a line behind it. When the pen is up, the catwon't.

In order to toggle between having the pen up and the pen down, we are going to require the code to remember which state the pen is in. Programs use variables to do this. A variable is a chunk of memory that allows you to place data in and read data from. Before you are going to be able to use a variable, you are going to have to tell the computer to assign memory to it. We are also going to assign it a name that we can use to refer to it in the commands.

Go to **Variables**, in the same area you found control and motion, click on **Make a Variable,** and give it the name **Pen**. Once you have done this, you are going to see a selection of commands that are able to alter or use the variable. Now that we have a way to store the date, we are going to tell the computer to change its behavior based on what the variable is. This is done using an **If... Else** block. This is going to ask if a statement is true. If it is, it will execute the first block of code. If not, it will execute the second.

In our program, we are going to take the variable, **Pen**. If it is 0, we are going to put the pen down, then set it to one. Otherwise, we will lift the pen and set it to be 0. In this way, we are going to be able to toggle between the two states by using the spacebar.

Now you can move the cat around and draw a picture. However, wouldn't it be even better if you could insert a predefined item? We are going to learn how to add circles next. Technically it is going to be a twenty-four-sided shape, but it will look similar to a circle.

The method to do this is to **move forward 10**, then **rotate 15 degrees**, then **move forward 10**, then **rotate 15 degrees**, and keep doing this until you have completed the circle, which would require you to put in the same two lines twenty-four times. This would work, but it isn't the best way. Not only would it look terrible in the coding and be time consuming, but if you wanted to change the size of the circle, you would need to do this twenty-four times. The good news is, there is a better option.

Instead of writing out the code twenty-four times, can instead use a loop. A loop is a block that repeats itself. There are different types of loops, some that will keep going until a statement becomes false, and some that execute a set number of times. For this, we are going to use one that executes a set number of times. You can find the loop option in the yellow control tab. We are going to use just two commands: **move forward 10**, and **rotate 15 degrees.** We will then set this to happen twenty-four times.

Now that you know how to use Scratch, you can play around with Scratch and discover just how much you can do with this programming software. (Peers, 2015)

Python

While Scratch is great to help you to learn the basics of programming, sooner or later you are going to reach its limitations and want to move onto something new. Python is a popular general-purpose programming language that is also easy to learn.

The first thing you need to be aware of is that Python is entirely text-based. This doesn't mean that it is unable to create graphics, but rather that your program code is going to written text instead of the drag and drop blocks we used in Scratch.

Before you get started with Python, it is important to know that since Python is text-based, you can use any text editor to create your programs. Leafpad comes with Pi and is a great starting point. Avoid using word processors such as LibreOffice Writer as they mess up the formatting and won't allow your program to function correctly.

First, open the Pi **menu** and choose **Programming** and then **Python 3**. This is the command line, but since we want to access

IDLE's text editor, we are going to choose **File** and **New** to create a new blank document. On the first line type:

#!/usr/bin/python

This line is going to tell the system to use the program python, in the folder /usr/bin/ to run the file. This is important to add to the start of all the programs you create with Python.

In the programming world, there is a long-standing tradition of having your first program output "Hello World!" and we aren't going to break it here! Leave the second line blank and on the third line type:

Print "Hello World!"

Save your work in a file called hello.py. Skipping a line in your coding is not strictly necessary. However, it makes your code easier to read.

To run the program we just created, open a terminal and navigate to where you saved the file. The default will be your home folder. First, type the following command to tell the system the file is executable:

$ chmoda+x hello.py

Next, type this command to run your program:

$ ./hello.py

You should see Hello World! appear on the screen. This shows us that the system is running properly. However, this program is not a very useful program.

(Peers, 2015)

Like we did with Scratch, we are going to add some user input. With the Python program, we are going to need to add a variable to store what the user types are. Delete the line with Hello World, leaving the top line, and add the line:

Name = raw_input('what is your name')

This line is going to create the variable name, display the prompt, "what is your name?", and store what the user types are. We must place this in inverted commas so the computer can recognize it as a single chunk of text. We are then going to be able to use this variable to make our print statement a little more personal with the line:

print 'Hello', name

Since the computer is going to run the commands in order, this one needs to be below the previous one. If you were to reverse the order they are in, the computer will register an error because we are trying to use a variable before we have even created it. You can now save the file and enter **./hello.py** at the command line to run the program.

This makes the program more functional, but leaves it relatively lifeless. In order to make it more useful, we need to add a step where the computer must look at what was inputted and perform a different task based on that input. If you recall the **If** block in Scratch, we are going to do something similar here except, we are actually going to write the code. The basic structure is going to be:

if :

code block

This must be replaced with something that can be true or false. In our case, we are going to check if the name entered is a particular value:

If name == 'Jane' :

Why ==? Computers don't deal well with ambiguity. Every symbol or word that we use can only have one meaning. Otherwise, things start to get confusing. The equal sign, "=", is used to assign a value to a variable, so we need to use something else to check the equality. Again, we are going to enclose **Jane** in inverted commas so the computer can recognize it's text. The colon tells the computer that we have finished our expression, and we are about to tell it what to do.

We may want this **If**command to run through more than one line of code. This means that we need a way to group code into blocks. This is done using indents in Python. Indents can be either a space or a tab. However, it is crucial to use the same method throughout your project to avoid confusion. Python doesn't read the amount of indentation, but rather the number of indents you have made. Personally, I use two spaces for each indent, because that's how I was taught, and it makes it simple to keep it all the same.

Back to our programming. Now we want the computer to do something **if name == 'Jane'** so we have to tell the computer what we want it to do.

if name == 'Jane' :

print "Jane, you're awesome"

Note that there are two spaces at the start of the second line. There are also double speech marks. This is because the text we have enclosed has an apostrophe in it. Since we don't want to be rude to all the people who aren't Jane, we are going to add an else block that runs whenever the above expression is false:

else :

print 'hello', name

One last feature we are going to include is a

loop. This is going to work similar to the one we created in Scratch, except it isn't going to only run twenty-four times. Instead, it will run until we tell it to stop. We are going to do this using a while look and the syntax:

while :

code block

We can have the program stop by entering the **name quit**. This means our **while** loop will be:

while name !: 'quit' :

For some reason, exclamation marks are often used to mean "not in the programming world". However, we are still left with a bit of a problem. If we put it before **name = raw_input...** we are going to produce an error because the computer doesn't know what **name** is. But if we put it after, it will only ask us to enter a name once, then spit the greeting out indefinitely, which is also not ideal.

There is a way to solve this. We are simply

going to string the name before **while**. This stops the error and will always trigger the **while** expression. So, the program should look like this:

```
#!/usr/bin/python

name = "

while name != 'quit' :
name = raw_input('What is your
name?')

if name == 'Jane' :
print "Jane, you're awesome"
else :
print 'Hello', name
```

You should note that there are four spaces before each print line. This is because they have been indented twice. Once for the **while** loop and once for the **if** statement. Now you can save this as hello.py and as before, run it with ./hello.py.

Both Scratch and Python are great programs to get started with, so now you can pick the one that appealed to you the most. In the next chapter, we are going to look at some sample project ideas that you can use to get started with programming your Raspberry Pi 3 – Model B.

Chapter 6: Sample Project Ideas For Your Raspberry Pi

Now you know all the technical information about your Raspberry Pi 3 – Model B, as well as some of the basics about using it for programming. From here we are going to go over some sample projects you can do, or build off of, as you begin to learn all that your Raspberry Pi can do.

Turn Your Raspberry Pi into A Wireless Access Point

There are many different reasons you might want to turn your Raspberry Pi into a wireless access point. Here are some of the most common reasons:

- Extend your existing Wi-Fi Network;

- Learn more about wireless networking;

- Create a free Access Point;

- Build a honey trap to learn about network hardening;

- Learn about sniffing packets;

- Provide guest wireless access that is firewalled through your main network;

- Closed Wi-Fi monitoring station for weather recording, temperature sensing; and

- Create a Raspberry Pi Hot Spot.

The first thing you need to do is ensure that your Raspberry Pi 3 – Model B is all set up and ready to be used. Assuming that it is, you are now going to run **sudoraspi-config** and set up your Pi, changing your memory split to sixteen. You are then going to reboot and set a password, if you choose to, for the root user. Assuming that you are logged in under Root User, you are now going to install Aptitude with **apt-get install aptitude**. Once this is installed, you are going to use the command **aptitude update; aptitude safe-upgrade**. The speed of your internet is what will determine how long this process is going to take.

Once that has finished, you are going to install a few packages:

Aptitude install rfkill zd1211-firmware hostapd-utilsiwdnsmasq

These are:

rfkill – Wireless utility

zd1211-firmware – Software for dealing with zd1211 based wireless hardware

hostapd – This is the hostap wireless access point

hostap-utils – These are the tools that go with hostap

iw – Wireless configuration utility

dnsmasq – A DHCP and DNS utility

An addition option is to add **vim** to that list. Vim is a nicer console editor than the default vi. Next, you are going to locate the file /etc/dhcpcd.conf. Once you have found this file, you are going to add these lines to the end:

interface wlan0

staticip_address=192.168.1.1/24

static routers=192.168.0.1

staticdomain_name_servers=8.8.8.8
8.8.4.4

These lines are going to instruct dhcpcd to statically configure the WLAN0 interface with an IP address. You can change this IP address to whatever you are intending to use for your wireless network. However, you must leave the /24 as it is important and the coding will not work without it. At this time, you should change the gateway from the default 192.168.0.1 to whatever the gateway is on your normal LAN which the wired ETH0 interface is connected to. Leave the domain_name_servers as is, that's the Google DNS farm and should always work.

The next thing we are going to do is configure hostap. We are going to edit /etc/hostapd/hostapd.conf to look like this:

interface=wlan0

driver=nl80211

ssid=test

channel=1

Ensure that you don't leave any spaces at the end of each line, as hostap is very literal in reading its configuration and spaces will alter how the language is being read.

Finally, you are going to configure dnsmasq to allow yourself to obtain an IP address from your new Pi Point. Edit /etc/dnsmasq.conf to look like this:

 # Never forward plain names (without a dot or domain part)

domain-needed

 # Only listen for DHCP on wlan0

interface=wlan0

 # create a domain if you want, comment it out otherwise

#domain=Pi-Point.co.uk

 # Create a dhcp range on your /24 wlan0 network with 12 hour lease time
dhcp-
range=192.168.1.5,192.168.1.254,255.255.255.0,12h

 # Send an empty WPAD option. This may be REQUIRED to get windows 7 to behave.
#dhcp-option=252,"\n"

Remember that you are going to change the dhcp-range to match the network IP address you are using. To ensure that your Pi Point is going to work after it is rebooted, you are going to need to create a run file that will turn on forwarding, nat and run hostap at the time of booting. To do this you are going to create a file named /etc/init.d/pipoint with the following contents:

#!/bin/sh
 # Configure Wifi Access Point.
#

```
### BEGIN INIT INFO
# Provides: WifiAP
# Required-Start: $remote_fs $syslog
$time
# Required-Stop: $remote_fs $syslog
$time
# Should-Start: $network $named
slapdautofsypbindnscdnslcd
# Should-Stop: $network $named
slapdautofsypbindnscdnslcd
# Default-Start: 2
# Default-Stop:
# Short-Description: Wifi Access Point
configuration
# Description: Sets forwarding, starts
hostap, enables NAT in iptables
### END INIT INFO
# turn on forwarding
echo 1 > /proc/sys/net/ipv4/ip_forward
# enable NAT
iptables -t nat -A POSTROUTING -j
MASQUERADE
```

 # start the access point

hostapd -B /etc/hostapd/hostapd.conf

Next make the script executable with **chmod +x / etc/init.d/pipoint** and add the script to the startup sequence of the Raspberry Pi using **update-rc.dpipoint start 99 2**. This will ensure that your Pi Point will reboot itself as a functioning Wi-Fi access point.

Turn Your Raspberry Pi 3 – Model B Into A Retro Arcade Machine

Who doesn't love retro video games? This project is going to show you how to very simply turn your Raspberry Pi into a retro games console in no time.

First, open up a terminal window. You can find this at the top of the screen. Once it's open, type **sudo apt-get update** followed by **sudo apt-get install -y git dialog**. Next, you are going to type **cd** and then **git clone git://github.com/petrockblog/RetroPie-**

Setup.git. This is going to download a little script that is going to install tons of game emulators for you. To prepare the installer, type: **cd RetroPie-Setup**, then **chmod +x retropie_setup.sh**.

In the same terminal window, we are going to type: **sudo./retropie_setup.sh**, this is going to run the installer and bring up an awesome retro interface. Once we are here, we are going to select the binaries-based install option. This is going to take about an hour.

Once this is installed, we are going to open up another terminal window and type: **sudoraspi-config**. In this configuration app, you are going to go into the boot options and choose to make the Pi boot into a command prompt instead of Raspbian. Now you are going to to reset the Pi, and then type **EmulationStation** to run your new retro game center.

This is going to give you access to emulators for

more than twenty systems, including the Mega Drive and Nintendo 64. While some games are going to be built in, you are going to have to check out a site like *emuparadise*.

Create A Media Center With Your Raspberry Pi

Before you get started on making your Raspberry Pi into a media center, you are going to need to obtain a few components:

- Raspberry Pi Case

- Standard SD card

- Micro-USB cable and wall charger

- HDMI cable

- USB mouse and keyboard

The first thing you are going to do is get your Raspberry Pi set up in the case. The board should fit snugly in the case without needing to be forced in. Once you have placed your Raspberry Pi into your case and screwed the top on, you are ready to move on.

The media center is going to run on RaspBMC Linux distribution, and you are going to need to download this from a computer other than the Raspberry Pi. Once you unzip the file, right click the file **setup.exe** and select "Run as Administrator" click yes to the User Account Control dialog. You will then be presented with an interface which will allow you to install the RaspBMC to an SD card. Next, select the SD card from the list and check the box stating that you agree with the license agreement and select install.

Now that the software has been installed on the SD card, you are going to insert it into the Raspberry Pi. Turn the Raspberry Pi on and begin the installation process. This can take up to forty-five minutes.

Now that RaspBMC has been installed, you are going to be given the option to choose a language, and will then be greeted with the home screen. Scroll over to the program section and select the RaspBMC settings option. This is going to allow you to change your connection type from wired to wireless. You are going to be able to change many other settings to personalize your experience.

Now you are ready to add your media. Since it is impractical to store your media on the SD card, we are going to be streaming the media from an existing computer.

Go to the home menu and navigate to the video option. Here, you should see a drop-down option for files, choose this option and then click the option to add videos. This should give you a menu that allows you to browse for a source.

Select browse. A screen will appear that contains a variety of options to connect. XBMC facilitates a number of different connection options. However, most computers are going to rely on the Windows Samba option, which you will find near the bottom. Once you have clicked on this option, it is going to ask you for the username and password for the computer you are trying to stream from. Enter this information, and you will be able to view the files that you have chosen to share. Now that you have added your media, you should be able to select the media and begin streaming content.

There are three different methods you can use to control the device you have just created.

1 – A wireless mouse is one option, although it is also the most inconvenient.

2 – There are various apps you can get for your Android or iPhone.

3 – A universal remote. This is the most ideal option since you likely already have one of

these in your home.

There are many, many more things you can do with your new Raspberry Pi 3 – Model B. We've walked through two of the most popular, and easiest, things you can do. Below is a list of other things that your Raspberry Pi is capable of. Feel free to attempt any of these projects, or create one of your very own, the only limit with the Raspberry Pi is your imagination.

Other Raspberry Pi Projects

- Write your own game
- Make a Gameboy (advanced)
- Make a Kodi streamer
- Build a download hub
- Create a dedicated Minecraft machine
- Build a camera trap
- Build a case for your Raspberry Pi
- Control your stereo wirelessly
- Create your own cloud server
- Make a phone

- Make a PiRate radio station
- Build a smart beer fridge
- Make a PiCam
- Make a talking toy
- Make a bitcoin mining machine
- Create a tiny arcade
- Build your own virtual assistant, similar to Amazon's Alexa
- Build a Raspberry Pi laptop
- Stream PC games to the Pi
- Raspberry Pi music player
- Raspberry Pi photo frame
- Make a motion sensor
- Raspberry Pi security camera network
- Build a Samba server
- Create a smart mirror

As you can see, the options of what you can do with the Raspberry Pi are virtually endless. Choose a project to get started with, and remember, if something ever goes wrong, simply go back to the beginning and reprogram your Raspberry Pi as if it were brand new.

Chapter 7: Accessories For Your Raspberry Pi 3 – Model B

Costing only $35, the Raspberry Pi is a great price, and it also very basic. However, there are many accessories you can get for your Raspberry Pi if you want to spend the money. In this chapter, we are going to briefly look at some of the available accessories and the pros and cons of each one. We are also going to take a look at what you would get from each accessory, whether that be aesthetic, functionality or something else.

Raspberry Pi 3 Starter/Media Center Kit

– For anyone who is buying the Pi 3, particularly if it is the first Pi owned, a starter kit can be a huge benefit. It comes with a power supply, a case, an 8GB micro SD card, HDMI and Ethernet cables. It also includes NOOBs, Raspbian, and Kodi pre-installed.

HDMI to VGA Adapter – HDMI is very common. However, it's still not everywhere. If you have a monitor that is not HDMI enabled, or you just prefer VGA, this is one attachment that will make your life a lot easier.

Raspberry Pi Heatsink – The Raspberry Pi 3 – Model B produces heat. If you are going to be doing advanced projects, it is going to produce more heat. To extend the life of the processor, a heatsink is a great option.

Raspberry Pi Touchscreen – Touchscreens are everywhere, and if you are planning on making a Pi Phone or tablet, this is a great product to have. While most of the touchscreens you are going to find are only 480p, it is still better than a non-touch display.

Camera Module – Almost every device available these days has a camera. Adding a camera to your Raspberry Pi will allow you to use it as a video calling box, home security system or even as an actual camera.

Pi Sense Hat – There are some things you

probably never considered you might need. Like temperature sensors, humidity sensors and an LED sensor. The PiSense Hat also has an accelerometer, a magnetic sensor, a five-button joystick, and a barometer. This makes it an essential tool for many projects.

Adafruit RGB Matrix – If you are hoping to make a stunning light show, or just need a basic display to showcase things, this fully programmable color LED board is your ideal gadget.

AdafruitPerma Promo Hat – This is a basic tool that will allow you to create and test your own custom circuits for use in your projects.

PaPiRuseink Display Hat – This is perfect if you are looking for a basic display that isn't going to suck up a bunch of power. This display is great to display a calendar, clock, or thermometer.

Mini Wireless Keyboard And Mouse Touchpad – This is great if you don't want to keep your Pi connected to a mouse and keyboard all the time. You aren't going to want to use this when you are typing out long strands of commands. However, it is great if you are only typing a few sudo commands or small mouse movements.

<u>Cases</u> – There are many different cases you can get for your Raspberry Pi. From the simplest cases that are used just to protect your Raspberry Pi from the elements, to cases that include a touchscreen holder or even mount to a monitor.

As you can see, there are many different options for accessories for your Raspberry Pi. Most of the accessories you are going to find listed above are available for under one hundred dollars. This means that even if you choose to invest in a few of your favorites, you are still going to be spending less than you would be on a traditional computer, and you are going to be able to do so much more with it.

Conclusion

Now that you know the basics of the Raspberry Pi 3 – Model B, you are ready to venture out and start getting some hands-on experience with it. Remember, there is a ton of different software options that you can use when you are programming your Raspberry Pi, so you are by no means confined to the ones that came standard with the Raspbian that we downloaded in the walkthroughs.

Remember, the Raspberry Pi computers were created to give everyone an affordable option to learn about technology and how they can manipulate it. Use your imagination and enjoy the process of learning how to program your Raspberry Pi 3 – Model B to do virtually anything you want it to do.

I would like to thank you for downloading my book: *Raspberry Pi: The Blueprint for*

Raspberry Pi 3: Everything You Need to Know For Starting Your Own Projects. I hope you found the content in this book to be a valuable contribution to what you are going to do with your Raspberry Pi.

Bibliography

Peers, B. E. (2015, December 29). Retrieved March 1, 2017, from http://www.techradar.com/news/software/learn-to-program-your-raspberry-pi-1148194

The Blueprint To Python Programming

A Beginners Guide: Everything You Need to Know to Get Started

By: CyberPunk Architects

Introduction

There are many people who are interested in getting into the world of coding. They want to learn some of the basics so that they can work on their own programs, learn how to work more on their own computers, or even get started on doing work for other people. But there are many different coding languages that you can learn to work with and sometimes this can be confusing to learn which is right for you. This guidebook is going to spend some time talking about the Python coding language, one of the best languages to learn as a beginner for its ease of use as well as all its power.

In this guidebook, you are going to learn about the Python coding language. We will start with some of the basics, including learning how to install the software, as well as the right IDE and text editor so that you are able to write some of your own code. We will then move on to some of the basics of this languagethat you would like to include inside your codes to make them work the best. And then we move on to handling the exceptions in Python, working with loops to get a block of code to repeat without having to rewrite it a bunch of times, and the conditional statements that will make decisions for you regardless of the answer that your user places into the code.

The Python language is one of the easiest coding languages to learn how to use. It is designed for the beginner with all of the power that you are looking for inside a new coding language. This guidebook is going to take some time to help you as a beginner learn more about coding with this language so you can create some of your own codes and really join the coding community.

Chapter 1: Getting to Know the Python Program

Getting started with a new programming language can be a bit scary. You want to make sure that you are picking out one that is easy to use so that you can understand what is going on inside of the program. But you may also have some big dreams of what you want to accomplish with the programming and want an option that is able to keep up with that. The good news is that the Python programming language is able to help with all of this and is the perfect coding language for a beginner to get started with.

There are many reasons why you would enjoy working with the Python language.It is easy to learn, is meant for beginners, and it works with some of the other coding languages that you may want to learn to add in more power. It is based on the English language so there are not going to be too many issues with learning difficult words, and it has a lot of the power that you need without all the complicated make-up of other coding languages. As you will see in a minute, the syntax in Python is really easy to learn and there are a lot of powerful things that you can do with this coding language, even as a beginner.

The Python library is going to be a great help to you as you get started with this language. It has many of the syntaxes and examples that you need to help you out when you get stuck or when you have some issues figuring out how to complete some steps in Python. The community with this coding language is large as well, due to the fact that this is an easy code to work with and is great for beginners, so you will be able to find others to ask questions of or you can read through forums to learn more about the projects you want to work on.

If you are interested in getting started with the Python language, there are a few things that you will need to have on hand to make the process easier. First, you will need to make sure that the right text editor is in place on your computer. This is important because it is the software that you need to use in order to write out the codes to use inside of Python. The text editor doesn't have to be high end or complicated, and in fact, using the free Notepad option on any Windows computer, or another of this nature, will work just fine.

Once you have chosen the text editor that you would like to use, you will be able to download the actual Python program to use. The nice thing about this is that Python is free to download, as is the IDE and the other options that you will need, so you won't have to worry about the financial aspect of it. To get the Python program set up, you will just need to visit the Python website and choose the version that you would like to use.

While you are getting the Python program set up on your computer, you will also need to make sure that you download the IDE in the same instance. The IDE is basically the environment that you are going to be working in, and it will include the compiler that you need to interpret the codes that you are writing. It is often best to use the one that comes with the Python programming because this one is designed to work the best, but if you are used to working with a different IDE, you will be able to use that one as well.

If you find that there are times that you have questions about using this coding language, such as how to work on a particular code or if you are lost about why something isn't working, you should take the time to visit a Python community. The Python language has been around for some time, and it is one of the most popular coding languages in use, so the communities are pretty large. You should be able to find many groups of beginners and those who are more advanced who will be able to help you with your questions or any of the concerns that you have while learning this language.

Some of the basic parts of the Python code

Now that you have some of the Python software all set up and ready to go, it is time to work on some of the basics that come with this code. There are a lot of different parts that work together to write some amazing codes inside of Python, but learning about these basics will make it a bit easier to handle and when getting into some of the more complex processes later on. Here are some of the basics that we are going to concentrate on first before moving to some of the harder stuff later on:

Keywords

Any coding software that you use is going to have some keywords. These are words that will tell the interpreter what you want to happen in the code, so they are important to be familiar with. It is recommended that you do not use these anywhere else in your code in order to avoid confusion or error when the interpreter gets a hold of it, considering these are major action words. Some of the keywords that you should look at when working in the Python language include:

- False
- Finally
- Class
- Is
- Return
- Continue

- None
- For
- Try
- True
- Lambda
- Def
- Nonlocal
- From
- While
- Global
- Del
- And
- Not
- Raise
- In
- Except
- Break
- Pass
- Yield
- As
- If

- Elif
- Or
- Import
- Assert
- Else
- Import

This is a good list to keep on hand when you are writing your codes. This will help you to send the right information to the interpreter when you are writing through the code. Any time that you see an error message come up after writing out code make sure to check if you used one of those words properly within your statements.

Names of Identifiers

While working on a new code or program with Python, you will need to work with a few different things including variables, functions, entities, and classes. These will all have names that are also called identifiers. When you are creating the name of an identifier, regardless of the type you are working on, some of the rules that you should follow include:

- You should have letters, both lower case and upper caseworkare acceptable, the underscore symbol, and numbers. You are able to choose any combination of these as well. Just make sure that there are no spaces between characters.

- You can never start an identifier with a number. You are able to use something like "sixdogs," but "6dogs" would not be acceptable.

- The identifier should not be one of the keywords that were listed above, and there should never be one of the keywords inside of it.

If you do go against one of these rules, you will

notice that a syntax error will occur and the program will close on you. In addition to the rules above, you should ensure that the identifiers are easy to read for the human eye. This is important because while the identifier may follow the rules that were set out above, they can still have trouble when the human eye isn't able to understand what you are writing out.

When you are creating your identifier, make sure that you pick one that will be descriptive. Going with one that will describe what the code is doing or what the variable contains is a good place to start. You should also be wary of using abbreviations because these aren't always universally understood and can cause some confusion.

Chapter 2: Some of the Basic Commands You Should Know in Python

In addition to the things that we discussed above pertaining to the Python language, there are some other things that you can put into your codes to make them really strong. There are many options and functions that you can incorporate into the codes in order to do things like: tell other programmers what to do inside the code, add similar parts with the same characteristics together, and so much more. Let's take some time to look at the different commands that you are able to use in your codes with Python and what they all mean.

Comments

Comments are a great thing to know how to use inside of Python. They allow you to leave little notes inside of the code for yourself or for other coders who want to take a look at what you are doing. The compiler is set up to not recognize these comments, this way you are able to put in as many comments as you would like without it affecting how the code is going to execute.

Python makes it really easy to add in these comments. You will simply need to use the "#" sign in front of the comment that you want to leave inside the code. Once you are done with the comment that you want to leave, you just need to hit the return button and start out on a new line so that the compiler knows that you are starting on a new part of the code. As mentioned, you are able to leave as many of these little notes inside of your code as you would like, but try to keep them just to the ones that are needed in order to keep the code looking nice and organized.

Statements

Another thing that you are able to add into your code is statements. Whenever you are working on a code, you will need to leave these statements inside of your code so that the compiler has some idea of what you would like to have shown up on the screen. A statement is going to basically be a unit of code that you can send over to the interpreter. Then your interpreter will look at the statement that you want to use and then execute it based on the command that you are giving it.

When you work on writing the code, you can choose how many statements you are able to write at one time. You can choose to just have one statement that is inside of your code, or you can have several of them based on what you would like to have happen inside of the code. As long as you keep the statements inside of the brackets inside the code and you use all the correct rules when you are writing out that part of the code, you will be able to include as many of these statements as needed into the code.

When you choose to add in a statement (or more than one statement) into the code, you will send it through to the interpreter, which is then going to work to execute the commands that you want, just as long as you make sure that you put everything else in the right place. The results of your statements will then show up on the screen when you execute it, and you can always go back in and make changes or adjustments as needed. Let's look at an example of how this would work when using statements in your code:

x = 56
Name = John Doe
z = 10

print(x)
print(Name)
print(z)

When you send this over to the interpreter, the results that should show up on the screen are:

56
John Doe
10

It is as simple as that. Open up Python and give it a try to see how easy it is to just get a few things to show up in your interpreter.

Working with variables

Variables are a good thing to learn about the inside of the Python code because they can be used to store your code in specific parts of your computer. So basically, you will find these variables are just spots on the memory of your computer that will be reserved for the values of the code that you are working on. When you are working on the variables in the code, you are telling the computer to save some room on its memory to store these variables. Depending on what type of data you would like to use in the code, the variable is able to tell the computer what space should be saved on that location.

Giving the variable a value

In order to make the variables work inside the code, you need to make sure that they get a value assigned to each. Otherwise they are just basic places on the memory. You need to put some kind of value to the variable in order to get it to work properly, so it reacts inside the code. There are two types of variables that you will be able to use, and the one that you choose will determine the value type that you give to it. The different types of variables that we can pick from include:

Float: this would include numbers like 3.14 and so on.

String: this is going to be like a statement where you could write out something like "Thank you for visiting my page!" or another similar phrase.

Whole number: this would be any of the other numbers that you would use that do not have a decimal point.

When you are using this program, you will not need to use declarations in order to reserve this space on the memory since this is something that will occur right when you add a value to the variable you are working with. If you want to make sure that this is going to happen automatically, you just need to use the (=) symbol so that the value knows which variable it is supposed to be working with:

Some examples of how this works include:

x = 12   *#this is an example of an integer assignment*

```
pi = 3.14        #this is an example of a floating
point assignment
customer name = John Doe        #this is an
example of a string assignment
```

Now at this point, we are looking at just writing the code, but what if you would like to have the interpreter execute the code that we are using. Luckily, this is pretty simple to work on. You just need to make sure that you write out the word "print" before the statement that you want to use. However, in the newer versions, such as Python 3, you would want to add in the parenthesis. Either way, this is pretty easy to learn how to do. Here is a good example of how you would be able to make this work inside Python:

```
print(x)
print(pi)
print(customer name)
```

Based on the information listed above, when this is printed out, your interpreter is going to execute the results:

12

3.14

John Doe

You are also able to add in more than one value to the same variable if this is what needs to happen for the code to work within your code. You just need to make sure that you are including the equal sign ("=") in between each of the parts to make it work the right way. For example, "a = b = c = 1" would be acceptable and makes it so that all of those variables would equal 1 inside of your code. This is just a simpler option to use rather than writing each of these out on their own and making them equal to 1.

These are just a few more of the basics that you

will need to learn how to use when it comes to writing out your own codes in Python. These are pretty simple to learn how to do and you are going to enjoy all the power that they add into even the simplest codes you will be writing in the beginning.

Chapter 3: Working with Loops in Python

Now that we know some of the basics associated with working on the Python language, it is time to move into some of the more complex parts of this language and learn how to make it all work for your program. With the other options included in this guidebook, we talk about decision control instructions or sequential control instructions. When we are working with the decision control options (which will be discussed in the following chapter), we are putting the calculations into a fixed order to be figured out.With the sequential option, the interpreter is going to execute your instructions based on how your conditions will turn up at the end. There are a few limitations that come up with these options, mostly because they are only able to do the action once.

Now, what happens if you would like to have the action done more than once? With the other options that we discussed in this book, this would mean that you would need to rewrite the code over and over again until it is repeated as many times as you would like it to be. But what happens when you want to make something like a table that counts from 1 to 100? Do you want to write out the same part of code 100 times to make this happen?

Luckily, there are some options within Python that can be used to make it easier to write out these things as many times as you would like, while only taking up a few lines. These are called "loops," and they ensure that you are able to repeat the code as many times as you would like, from one to a thousand or higher if you would like. They are much easier to write out, they can save you a lot of time, and they will basically ensure that you are going to get the loop to continue until the conditions of the code are no longer true.

At first, you may feel that these loops are going to be kind of complicated because you have to tell the program how to repeat itself over and over as many times as you want, but it is actually pretty simple. There are three different types of loops that you can use inside of Python depending on what you would like the code to do. The three loops that you are able to use include the "while" loop, the "for" loop, and the "nesting" loop. Each of the loops is going to work in a different way to help you to repeat the part of the code that you need as many times as needed. Let's take a look at how each of these work, and when you would choose to use each one inside of your code.

What is the while loop?

The first loop that we are going to take a look at is the while loop. This is a good one to start on when you would like to make the code repeat itself, or go through the same actions, a fixed amount of times. For example, if you want to make sure that the loop goes through the same steps ten times, you would want to use the while loop.But if you would like to use this to create an indefinite number of loops, this is not the option to go with.

One of the examples that you would want to use with the while loop is when calculating out the amount of interest that is owed or paid. You can do this several times in order to find the perfect option for your user, but this one can be set up so that the user will not have to go back through the program multipletimes and get frustrated. Here is a good example that you can use in order to learn how the while loop statements are going to work when you would like to calculate simple interest:

#calculation of simple interest. Ask user to

input principal, rate of interest, number of years.

counter = 1
while(counter <= 3):
        principal = int(input("Enter the principal amount:"))
        numberofyeras = int(input("Enter the number of years:"))
        rateofinterest = float(input("Enter the rate of interest:"))
        simpleinterest = principal * numberofyears * rateofinterest/100
        print("Simple interest = %.2f" %simpleinterest)
        #increase the counter by 1
        counter = counter + 1
        print("You have calculated simple interest for 3 time!")

With this particular loop, the user will be able to put in the numbers they want to use for interest three times. After they are done, it will be set up to have a message show up on the screen. You can make this more complicated if you would like, adding in more lines for the user to input their answer as many times as they choose. The user of the program will be the one in charge, choosing how much they want to put into each of the spots. The user will be able to redo this program as well, starting over at the beginning, if they would like to add in more than the three interest spots than what they have in right now.

Working with the for loop

Now that we understand a bit more about the while loop, it is time to move on to the for loop. This one will work similarly to the other loop, but is a more traditional way to work with loops.If you have worked in any other coding languages in the past, you may be more familiar with this particular loop. If you do plan to use

Python with another coding language, you should consider using the for loop to make things easier.

When using the for loop, the user will not be the one who defines the conditions that will make the loop stop. The Python program is going to make the statement continuerepeating, in the exact order that it is placed inside your statement. Below you will find an example of how the for loop would work inside your code:

```
# Measure some strings:
words = ['apple','mango','banana', 'orange']
for w in words:
print(w, len(w))
```

Take some time to insert these statements into your compiler. With this one, the four fruits that are in this code, or the other statements that you choose to use, will repeat in the order that you write them out. If you are writing out this particular code and you want to make sure that they come out in a different order than what is listed above, you will need to make sure that you turn them around when writing the code. The computer will not take the time to make the changes and it is not going to allow you to change these at all when you are working on the actual code.

On the other hand, if you are looking for the loop to just go through a certain sequence of numbers or words, such as only wanting the first three fruits to show up on the screen, you will find that using your range() function is the best one for this. This function is going to generate a big list of the arithmetic progressions that you can use inside of the code to help make this easier.

The nested loops

The third type of loop that we are going to take

a look at is the nested loop. This one is going to sound a bit more complicated than you are used to with the other two options, but the code is actually going to be shorter than the others, and all the options that you are going to be able to do with the nested loop can make it a great one to learn even as a beginner. To keep things basic, the nested loop is just a loop that is inside of another loop. Both of the loops will just keep going through the repeat process until both of the programs have time to finish.

We are going to take a moment to look at an example of working on the nested loops. We are going to use the idea of a multiplication table in order to show you how several loops inside your code will be able to bring up a lot of information and you will only need to have a few lines of code to make this happen. The code that we are going to write will make the multiplication table go from 1 up to 10. Here is the example that you are able to use:

#write a multiplication table from 1 to 10

For x in xrange(1, 11):

   For y in xrange(1, 11):

   Print '%d = %d' % (x, y, x*x)

When you get the output of this program, it is going to look similar to this:

1*1 = 1

1*2 = 2

1*3 = 3

1*4 = 4

1*5 = 5

This would continue going until you got all the way up to 1*10 = 2

Then it would move on to do the table by twos such as this:

2*1 =2

2*2 = 4

2*3 = 6

For this one, you are going to keep on going until you end up with 10*10 and the answer that goes with this. You will have a complete multiplication table without having to write out the lines that go with each one, which makes this whole process easier to handle. Just look at the code above, there are only four lines (one of which is a comment), and you can get a table that is pretty complete and long. This is just one of the samples of what you are able to do and one of the main reasons that people will choose to go with loops rather than trying to write out all of the lines that they need.

Loops are one of the best things that you can work on when it comes to being inside the Python language. It can simplify the code that you are working on and ensures that you are able to get a lot of stuff done inside the code without having too much information written out and making it look like a mess. Try out a few of these loop options in your code and see what a difference they can make.

Chapter 4: Handling Exceptions in Your Code

There are times when you will need to work with exceptions when working inside the code. These can work one of two ways. For the first one, it is an exception that the program doesn't like, such as trying to divide a number by zero. When this happens, an error is going to come up on the screen, but you will be able to change the message that comes up on the screen with this to help avoid issues and to make sure that your user has some idea of what the issue is. Then there are exceptions that are particular to your program. If you do not want to allow your user to put in a certain number or another input, you would want to raise an exception to make this not allowed.

So any time that you would like to show the user that a condition is considered abnormal within the code, you will want to bring out the exceptions. There are several types of these that show up inside of the code, and some of which are as simple as writing out the code the wrong way or using theincorrect spelling that will cause the errors.

Any time that you are working in your Python program, and you want to make sure that you are bringing up the exceptions in the proper way, you will want to check out the Python library. There are several of these exceptions that are already in place inside the library and will save you a lot of time.It can be extremely beneficial when you check these exceptions out first. There are several exception types that you are able to use inside this language, including whenever you are dividing a number by zero, or whenever you try to reach a part that is outside the end of the file.

Exceptions can be a nice thing to work with within Python. The nice thing is that you aren't stuck dealing with the error messages that come up on a code. You can change them up a bit to help explain what is going on to the user so that any confusion can be bypassed. When an error message comes up on the screen, it can be difficult to determine what is wrong, especially if your user has no experience working with coding at all. But when you can make some changes, such as adding in a message like "you are trying to divide by zero!" it can explain what is going on with the error so the user can correct or change their process,and makes your code a bit more user-friendly.

You are also able to make some of your own exceptions if the code you are writing asks for it. You will not be able to find these inside of the Python library, but it is still an option that you are able to use. You will need to create some of these on your own so that an error, which can be a message like you did with the ones that were found in the library, will make things easier for the user to understand why the error is showing up.

When you are trying to write out exceptions within the Python language, there are a few things that you are going to find inside of your Python library in which you should take a bit of time to look over and learn how to work with. If you would like to work on the exceptions, you will need to make sure that you learn some of the key terms that need to be present to tell the compiler what you are doing. There are many options to choose from, but some of the statements that are best for working inside of your code with exceptions inside of Python coding include:

- Finally: with this one, you will be able to bring up the word to do the cleanup actions. This is a good one to use whether the user brings up the exception or not.

- Assert: this is the condition that is used whenever you would like to trigger that an exception has occurred inside the code.

- Try/except: these are the keywords that you will want to use whenever you are trying out a block of code. It is going to be recovered because of the exception that was raised either by you or by the Python program for some other reason.

- Raise: when you use the raise command, you are working to trigger the exception outside the code, doing so manually.

These are some of the best words to use in order to work with your exceptions and to make sure also that you will get all of your errors and other parts to work within the code. Whether you want to raise an exception that is recognized by the code or you are trying to work with one that is just for your program, in particular, you will be able to use these to help make things work within the code.

Raising an exception

Now that we have taken some time to look at what exceptions are all about, it is now time to learn how to raise exceptions. This is a pretty easy concept for you to work on and understand. For example, whenever you are working with the code inside of Python, and there is some kind of issue that is coming up with it, or you see that the program is trying to do things that aren't allowed within the rules of Python, the compiler is going to raise an exception for the behavior in question. This is because the program is going to see the issue and will not be sure about how it should react.

In some cases, the exception that is going to be raised will be pretty simple and could be something like naming the code the wrong way or spelling something wrong. You will just need to go back through the code and make the changes. Or there could even be some issues with the user attempting an action that is not allowed by the code, such as when a user may try to divide by zero. Let's take a look at how this is going to work so that you can see the steps that are needed in order to raise an exception:

x = 10

y = 10

result = x/y #trying to divide by zero
print(result)

The output that you are going to get when you try to get the interpreter to go through this code would be:

>>>

Traceback (most recent call last):
File "D: \Python34\tt.py", line 3, in

<module>
      result = x/y
ZeroDivisionError: division by zero

>>>

For the example that we did above, the Python coding language is going to show an error because you were trying to take a number and divide it by zero. The Python language is one that won't allow you to do this action, and so the error is going to come up on the screen. As we mentioned above, when you see that this error is coming up, the user may be confused and not understand what is going on at all. When you use this to raise up an exception, you should consider changing up the message so that the user has some idea of what is going on so that he or she can make the correct and necessary changes so that the code will work the way that it should.

How to make your own exceptions

So far, we have spent most of our time looking at the steps that you will need to take in order to work with the exceptions that are already recognized by the system. But what happens when you would like to raise some of your own exceptions that work with your particular programthat the system does not already recognize? A good example for this is when you want to make sure that your user is not able to place specific numbers into the system.You want to make sure that when the user places these numbers into the system, they are going to get an exception. Or if you would like the user to put in five numbers and they only put in four, you could use the idea of exceptions as well.

The trick with this type of action is that the Python program may not see that there is even an issue. The program is not going to realize that there is an issue with just putting in four numbers rather than the five unless you tell it that this is an issue. You will be the one who is able to set up the exceptions that you want to use, and you can mess around and add in any exception that you would like as long as it meets up with the other rules that are used inside of Python. Let's take a look at the example that is below so that we can understand how the exceptions work and to get some practice with using these:

```
class CustomException(Exception):
def_init_(self, value):
        self.parameter = value
def_str_(self):
        returnrepr(self.parameter)


try:
        raiseCustomException("This is a
CustomError!")
except CustomException as ex:
        print("Caught:", ex.parameter)
```

When you use this syntax, you will get the message of "Caught: This is a CustomError!" and any time that your user is on the program and puts in the wrong information, the error message is going to show up. This error is going to be caught if you put the conditions into the program the right way and it is important, especially if you set up your own exceptions in the code, that you place the conditions into the code.

It is possible to add in any wording as you would like into this part, so you can change it up as much as you would like to help better explain to the user what the error message means or what they may be doing wrong.. Mess around with this a little bit and you will find that it is easier than ever to set up some of your own exceptions or deal with the exceptions that are going on inside of your code.

Working with exceptions is a great way to ensure that you are getting the most out of your code. There are times when the code will see an abnormal condition and will need to put up a message or you will be working on your own program, and you will want to make up some of these abnormal conditions to work with what you are doing. Take a look at some of the examples that are done inside of this chapter, and you will be able to work with any of the exceptions that you would like in Python.

Chapter 5: Conditional Statements in Python

When it comes to working with your code, there will be times when you will want to make sure that the code is going to function in a specific way based on the conditions that you set,as well as the answer that the user puts in. You can keep it simple and have only one answer as an output when the user inputs an answer that is considered true based on your conditions, or you can make it more complex so that different answers will come up based on whether the input from the user is true or false.You can also give the user multiple options toinput,and they can choose from those. In this chapter, we are going to take some time to talk about the different conditional statements that will work inside the Python code, including the "if" statement, the "if else"statement and the "elif" statements.

The if statement

The first statement that we are going to work with inside of Python is the "if" statement. This is the most basic of the conditional statements, and it is often a good place to start when first learning code.But there will be some challenges when it comes to the user putting inan answer that does not agree with the conditions you set.

With the if statement, you must set the conditions and then the program will do the rest, waiting for the answer from the user. If the user puts in an answer that is considered true, based on the conditions that you set, the rest of the code will be executed. This is usually in the form of a statement of some sort showing up on the screen, and then the compiler moving on to the next part of the code. On the other hand, if the user puts in an answer that is not allowed or is considered false based on the conditions that you set, nothing is going to happen. The if statements are not set up for false answers, so the program will just stop at that point.

There are going to be some issues with this of course, but it is a good place to get started. This one will help you to see how the conditional statements are going to work and gets you some practice with the compiler, but we will look at some conditional statements that are able to look further into the work we are doing so that answers will show up regardless of the answers that are put in. Let's take a look at an example of working with the if statement to give you some practice.

age = int(input("Enter your age:"))
if (age <=18):
*   print("You are not eligible for voting,*
try next election!")
print("Program ends")

Let's take a look at this syntax a bit to see what

is going on. With this one, when the user comes onto the site and says that their age is under 18, they will match as true with the conditions that you set. This means that the statement that you put in, the "You are not eligible for voting, try next election!", will come up on the screen.

On the other hand, if the user puts in that they are another age, such as 25, into this code, nothing is going to happen. The if statement is not set up in order to handle this issue and there are no statements that are going to show up if this situation occurs. The compiler will just stop working on the code because it is false. You will need to make some changes to the code to handle this.

For the most part, you are not going to be able to use this type of conditional statement. The user is not wrong if they enter an age that is above 18 in the example above and they aren't going to really care for it if they can't see any results after they enter their age. How would you feel if you put in an answer to a program and it just stopped? The if statement is not the most efficient method of taking care of your conditional statements, so there will be many times that you should avoid using this at all. That is where the if else statement is going to come in handy.

If else statement

As we talked about above, there are some issues that come up when using the if statement. If your user enters an answer that is considered true with the if statement, the correct part of the code will execute.But if your user enters an answer that is seen as false (even if it is true for them), they will end up with a blank screen. This can easily end up with some problems when working within your code.

This is when the if else statement is going to

come in use. With this one, you are able to set up true and false conditions, and different parts of the code are going to be executed based on the answers that the user gives. Pertaining to the prior example, the user could receive an answer saying they are not able to vote if they say they are under 18.But if they input an answer of 30, they would get a second answer, such as information on their closest voting poll or another relevant piece of information.

The if else statement is going to allow for more freedom inside of your code. This makes it easier than ever before for you to handle whatever answer the user puts into the system, whether it is considered true or false. With this statement, the compiler will check the answer, and if it is seen as true for that particular one, it will execute that part of the code. But if not, it moves on to the second part of the code and executes that. You are able to expand on this, going down as many times as you would like if

you want to have several different answers.
Here is a good example of how you would be
able to use the if else statement inside of
Python:

```
age = int(input("Enter your age:"))
if (age <=18):
        print("You are not eligible for voting,
try next election!")
else
        print("Congratulations! You are eligible
to vote. Check out your local polling station to
find out more information!)
print("Program ends")
```

With this example above, there are basically
two options that you can use in the statement.
If the user puts in their age as being 18 or
younger, the first statement is the one that is
going to come up. So on the screen, they are
going to see the message "You are not eligible
for voting, try next election!" But if the user

puts in that they are 19 or above in age, they will see adifferent message that says: "Congratulations! You are eligible to vote. Check out your local polling station to find out more information!". This is a simple example that shows how the user will be able to put in any age that they want and the answer corresponding to their specific input is going to show up on the screen.

This one is a basic version of what you are able to do with the if else statement. This one just has one true, and one false answer and that is all that is on the statement. But there are times when you would like to have some options that the user can choose from, or you want there to be more than one true answer. For example, let's say that you would like to have the user put their favorite color. You could have five of the else statements with blue, red, yellow, green, and white. If the user puts in one of those five colors, the statement that is with that color will come up. Add in a break part that will catch all the other colors that your user may want to pick from so that an answer comes up no matter what answer they pick out.

The if else statements are able to add a lot of great things that you can use with your codes. It allows it to make a decision inside of the code based on the conditions that you set and the input that your user places into the code. It is nice to use the if else statements because you can better prepare for the various answers that your user will enter, no matter what they decide to answer, and you are all set to go.

The elif statements

One more conditional statement that we are going to talk about in this chapter is the elif statement. These are a bit different than the others, but they are nice to work with because they provide the user with a few choices that they can choose from. Each of your choices are going to have a statement or a part of the code that will execute based on the decision that your user decides to go with. If you are creating a game and would like to make sure that the user can pick from several options before going further on, the elif statement is the one that you should use. The syntax that you would want to use with the elif statement includes:

if expression1:
statement(s)
elif expression2:
statement(s)
elif expression3:
statement(s)
else:
statement(s)

This is the basic syntax that you will want to work with whenever you want to use the elif statements in Python. You can just add in some of the information that you want so that the user can see the choices and pick the numbers that they would like to go with it, or the statements that work with their choices. This is one that you will be able to expand out a bit as you need, and you can choose to have two or three options or twenty options based on what you would like to see happen with the elif statements.

Here, we are going to take some time to look at how the elif statement is able to work in your coding. With this option, we are going to list a few choices of pizzas that the user is able to pick from and the corresponding number that they are able to work with. You can always add in some more options as well, and we add in an else part that is able to catch all the other options or, in this option, that will allow them to get a drink instead of a pizza if they do not like the options that are presented to them. Let's take a look at how this would be written out in your Python compiler:

```
Print("Let's enjoy a Pizza! Ok, let's go inside Pizzahut!")
print("Waiter, Please select Pizza of your choice from the menu")
pizzachoice = int(input("Please enter your choice of Pizza:"))
if pizzachoice == 1:
        print('I want to enjoy a pizza napoletana')
elifpizzachoice == 2:
        print('I want to enjoy a pizza rustica')
elifpizzachoice == 3:
        print('I want to enjoy a pizza capricciosa')
else:
        print("Sorry, I do not want any of the listed pizza's, please bring a Coca Cola for me.")
```

This is a pretty simple example of the elif statement and how you would be able to incorporate it into your codes. You can easily change this up to work with whatever program or game that you would like to create. The syntax, as you can see above, is offering the user a few options of pizzas that they are able to choose. When they are using the code, they will be able to pick the number that they would like and that corresponds to the pizza they want to go with. For example, if they would like to get the pizza napoletana, they would type in the number one. If they pick number one, they would see the answer "I want to enjoy a pizza napoletana" come up on their screen. This works for any of the numbers that they would chooseon this option. With this one, we have even set it up so that the user can choose to just have a drink without a pizza if this is what they prefer.

The if statements are one of the best options for

you to work with. They allow the code to come up with its own decisions based on the conditions that you set up in the beginning. You can make it as simple as the code just choosing to show a result when the user input is the same as your conditions, or you can add in some other parts to match up with the answers that the user places inside the code or with the choices that they want to make. There are many things that you are able to work with when using the conditional statements and you can make them as complicated or as simple as you would like.

Conclusion

Thank you for downloading *The Blueprint to Python Programming: A Beginners Guide to Everything You Need to Know to Get Started.*

The next step is to download the program and start writing some of your very own code. Since Python is a popular coding language and is great for beginners, it won't take long for you to get started on your first projects. This guidebook provided a few great examples that you can try out to get familiar with the system, but with the help of the knowledge you gained inside and the Python community, you will be writing great codes in no time. From learning how to write out the basic syntax in Python to working with conditional statements, operators, and variables, you are well on your way to being an expert in no time.

Finally, if you found this book useful in anyway,

a review on Amazon is always appreciated!

Free Bonus!

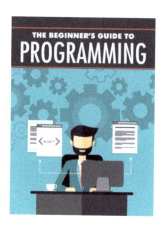

Programing can be hard but it doesn't have to be! Take this free PDF guide to understand some of the basics of programming

Download the free guide:

bit.ly/cpfreeguide

www.ingramcontent.com/pod-product-compliance
Lightning Source LLC
Chambersburg PA
CBHW041637050326
40690CB00026B/5247